Poetry from A Pleiadian

by

Lady Wise

Poetry from A Pleiadian

ISBN: 978-0-9933513-6-5

EBook: 978-0-9933513-7-2

The content of this book is intended to inform, entertain and provoke your thinking. This is not intended as medical advice, financial or any other kind of advice. That is your choice. It is your life and potential in your hands. The intent of the author is only to offer words of a general nature to help you in your quest for inspirational and spiritual upliftment. Neither the author nor the publisher can be held responsible or liable for any loss or claim arising from the use or the misuse of the content of this book.

Published by Lady Wise
Typeset by Raspberry Creative Type

Poetry from A Pleiadian

by

Lady Wise

Introduction

Aloha Mahalo!

Thanks in advance for reading my poems
May they inspire you in your own reality
Live for your dreams to manifest
And believe in their potentiality
Embrace this opportunity to celebrate all the good things
Stay grounded, be authentic for the adventures life brings!

"

Poetry
was the way of communication
of adventures of mankind.
~ Kryon

Mahalo Kokua!

With love and gratitude,

Lady Wise ♡

@LadyWiseWorld
www.ladywiseworld.com

Dedication

To all of my Akashic ancestors for your ongoing
love, support and benevolence
In everything I do from a place of love and magnificence

Here's to all of you across time and space
As we evolve in our consciousness to become a quantum race!

Acknowledgements

Special thanks to Lee Carroll and the support entity Kryon helping in the evolution of humanity at this time, for giving me permission to share some of their esoteric knowledge and wisdom with you as I have come to understand it and expressed this in my esoteric poems.

Enjoy listening to free audio channelled through Lee Carroll from the support entity Kryon available at https://www.kryon.com to further enhance your inner guidance system.

Contents

Section 1
Foodie Fun!

This first section covers those poems that I have written inspired by all kinds of food
To omit such delicacies and gourmet dishes would simply be rude
Seek to embrace new tastes and culinary challenges with positive attitude!
Perhaps adopt a different perspective on your food with kindness and gratitude?

POEM #1

Fromage

Distinctive cheeses, impressive selection, there's no mistaking the French connection
Delicious varieties, tastiest bites, cheeses from France have a way to delight
Finest quality, range and flavour, there's always a cheese for you to savour
Chaumes, Creamy Rambol, Brie, Camembert... other cheeses simply cannot compare
An excellent range, matured to perfection puts fromage savoir-faire on my cheese board selection
For texture, value, taste and tradition, fine cheeses from France defy competition
Creamy French cheese and classic red wine is a combination that is simply divine
When fromage abounds and Bordeaux flows, the mix is infectious and anything goes!
French cheese, fine wine and fresh baguette – how authentic can you get?
Such distinctive flavours all taste sublime, bringing out the best in French bread and wine
From bistro snack to gourmet venue, real French cheeses enhance the menu
A sumptuous meal without French cheese is like a sensual kiss without a squeeze
With over three hundred tasty cheeses from which to choose is it any wonder one can become most confused?
Oh yes, and French cows know the secret, but they won't grass!

POEM #2

Festive Food

Sparkling decorations light up my table like the star that shone over Bethlehem's stable
My mind turns to thoughts of Christmas catering, all those long queues and the tiredness from waiting
But less time spent in boring queues would leave more time to enjoy tasty food and booze
'Tis the season to be jolly', not pushing along a heavy trolley!
No stress, no hassle, worry-free, an ordering service would be perfect for me
Decking halls, hanging holly, with pre-ordered food I'd have time to be jolly
A joyous, happy Christmas beckons if I order the food for the 22nd
For the most wonderful festive dishes an ordering service fulfils all my wishes
I pick up the phone and press the digits; my order is placed in a matter of minutes
From parsnips to sprouts, festive joints to a dessert supreme, this ordering service is setting standards seldom seen
For first class taste, this Christmas treat has delicious aromas that nothing can beat
Excellent food, cooked to perfection, unrivalled choice with such varied selection
Convenient, versatile and nutritious, it's a "Claus" for celebration 'Oh so delicious!'
Peace on earth and good-fill to all!

POEM #3

A Sparkling Pair

Best bubbly, scrumptious sweet – without them a celebration is incomplete
Boisterous buffet party or intimate dinner, this combination's a sure-fire winner
A tasteful twosome oozing class has all the grandeur none can surpass
Such 'Foodie Fun' of superior class served up one in a dish and one in a glass
A long lasting affair, such a cool crisp, sparkling pair
Alluring, delicious, luxurious, beguiling – the perfect duo to keep you smiling
Rich, cool and ostentatious, they make every celebration event outrageous
Ice cream and champagne hand-in-hand epitomise perfectly why life is grand!

POEM #4
Fizzically Superior

For picnics, barbecues, sunshine and leisure, a glass of champagne adds sparkle to pleasure
Seductive, sensual, fruity and pure, this grape-filled drink boasts effervescent allure
A sparkling sensation lingers on my lips as I indulge in summer sips
It enlivens a party, enhances a date, on anyone's scale it's classed first rate
For toasts, speeches and exhilarating fun, a glass of champagne is second to none
Exciting, elegant, exceptionally fine, it's a perfect aperitif or party wine
Refreshing taste, bubbles explode; it puts everyone into summer season mode
With bubble and fizz just like laughter, the lasting enjoyment is just what I'm after
A glass of champagne designed to excite, tickles taste buds with delight
With delicious champagne I can party away, from New Year's Day till Hogmanay
Making me tingle from my head to my toes, all year round the fun just flows
Sparkling choice, taste bud titillation, this is a liquid asset in any location
Not since Eve's forbidden fruit has this become a desirable substitute
A winning beginning, the taste of tomorrow, its 'fizzical' superiority no others can follow
Bright and bubbly just like laughter, with happy memories the morning after.

POEM #5

A Rising Bubble

Pop, Pop and Away
Merci Air Fantastique
A Cru with a View
C'est Magnifique!
Sup, Sup and Away
Dizzy Fizzy
Fizzy Dizzy
Brut 'n Breezy
Fizzible Difference
Bubble Over
Affordable, stylish, tasting sublime – it's top of the pops every time!

POEM #6
Oranges

Paradise lost becomes paradise found with my favourite fruit growing all around
Satsumas and clementines, both citrus quenchers, peel back their skin for sun-kissed adventures
Soaked in sunshine, tended with care, there's nothing more natural anywhere
Full of goodness, juicy and sweet, sunshine fruit is so delicious to eat
There's no need to put yourself under pressure for these tangy fruits are the perfect refresher
Fiesta, siesta, sun, fun and "C", they are from the happiest, healthiest citrus family
Sunshine grown to family tradition, wholesome, delicious and full of nutrition
With warming sun and gentle breeze, these ripened oranges are picked to please
Fresh succulent citrus, varieties galore, packed full of sunshine, rushed straight to the store
They're easily a cut above the rest – overflowing with natural zest!
Sweetly priced with sunshine nutrition, they contribute to a luscious fruit bowl addition
Enjoy an orange as a health snack to help your immune system get back on track
With a daily intake of vitamin C, I start to observe a healthier me
Tempting and tasty enjoy orange as a drink, and before too long you'll feel in the pink

Mouth-watering entertainment, simply the best, squeezed full of flavour – an adventure in zest
Every sip's reminiscent of nature's beauty captured in juices fragrant and fruity!
It quenches thirst throughout the day in a flavourful calorie controlled way
Orchards, meadows, crisp country air, sipping orange juice takes me back there
It pampers the palate, mellows the mood, and perfectly complements everyday food
Always make time for a moment to treasure the perfect drink for work or leisure
Sheer enjoyment, perfect bliss, with a refreshing taste it's too good to miss
Taste a segment for a delicious sensation and know it's no figment of one's imagination!
Each 'C' packed segment gives vital nutrition, so enjoy and share your new found vision
Sip, savour, swallow, sigh – the perfect solution when feeling dry
Refreshed and quenched the purest way, inspiring picnic pleasures each day
Tangy fruits ripened by Spanish sunrays, make my taste buds shout, "Pip, Pip, Olé!"
100% pleasure, 100% pure, 100% enjoyment that's for sure
They're full of vitamins, "See!"

POEM #7

A Decent 'Porkposal'

Can you hog the barbecue without becoming a boar and
relax with a dinner that you'll adore?
For traditional medallions of tasty perfection why not buy a
cut of pork for your delectation?
A tender cut of saddle back's the "porkfect" aphrodisiac!
Delicious thick rashers served fresh on the table deliver a
sizzling meal with a quality label
Good value is naturally ensured when buying bacon that's
been traditionally cured
Consistently delicious, no chances taken, at least once a
week choose to bring home the bacon
From sty to fry, it's a perfect buy
There is no 'miss-steak', it's real meat not fake
If music be the food of love...oink, oink, oink!

POEM #8

Healthy Fare

Finest foods from home grown grains a healthy diet will sustain
Exceptional food from quality fields will contribute to farmers' superior yields
Harvest produce cannot be beaten, for tastiest food ever eaten,
From this green and pleasant land, quality and choice go hand in hand
Fresh from the farm to one's dinner table, quality assured comes with a quality label
Healthy cuisine at affordable cost will retain my good health with minimal financial loss
Greater value 'per pound' must be guaranteed if supermarkets are to succeed
Wholesome products nutritious and cheap are benefits from which all can reap
Sumptuous flavours at a budget price are the antidote to the spice of life
Oh for the widest choice in every store of home grown food – let's have more!
Quality produce packed with nutrition make healthy fare a steadfast British tradition
May the output of British country mills increase so that more individuals can enjoy the feast
Breakfast, lunch, dinner, tea – food from Britain is a good choice for me.

POEM #9

Beer

Microbrewers demonstrate focused dedication when it comes to the artisans' niche of beer fermentation
Could sipping beers from every nation be considered the ultimate taste-bud delectation?
Whatever the country and location this great occupation has no limitation
But it's thirsty work choosing satisfying beers, especially from both northern and southern hemispheres!
Nationwide pride bottled or canned, although languages differ, I understand!
Tasty ale, dark or pale, easily selected from a world-wide trail
Supreme beers sourced and savoured from many nations quench my thirst for dream vacations
Each country's own unique brew creations offer intoxicating diversity across the league of nations
The pick of Oktoberfest's delights transport me to Munich's visitor sights!
A Japanese craft beer brewed to perfection is the finest of eastern among the selection
With distinctive flavours perfected through time, award winning craft beers are quite sublime
Why would you back-pack when you can six-pack?
It's always first come, thirst served!

POEM #10
Darling Spuds

Perfect meals delight in every way when accompanied with
the "darling spuds of May"
With beautiful fresh taste and edible skin, it's guaranteed
there will be no waste for the bin
It's no fluke, you know, that soil, sun, sea and a little
tender care, produce an abundance of grand potatoes
extraordinaire
The mighty King Edward is quite a stunner; I believe one
swallow does indeed make a summer
There is nothing quite like them under the earth as they grow
to scrumptious beauties from their fledgling birth
They're succulent and heartily delicious, to crown it all,
extremely nutritious
So next time you're bewildered to know what to eat,
consider these darling spuds as a treat!

POEM #11

Fruit Loaf for Tea!

Pure ingredients, premium grade fruits, these are a world apart from alternative substitutes
I simply love stomach satisfying fruit loaf slices with sweet sensational seductive spices
Filled with taste explosions and raisins galore, there's no better loaf from my cupboard store
With focused senses, my palate to suit, I indulge in this gratifying loaf with harvested fruit
Although there are many raisins too numerous to mention, consuming more is my main intention!

POEM #12
Hot Cross Buns

Home-baked hot cross buns without a doubt leave something important to shout about
Temptingly tasty, meticulously made, they leave all imitations in the shade
Considered suitable for every occasion, fruity affair or spicy liaison
They welcome the promise of spring, with spices, sultanas and plenty of zing!
Whether they're eaten morning or night, it's a celebration of love at first bite
With their aromatic smell and gorgeous consistency, it's difficult not to resist them consistently
Their fruity wholesome flavour alerts senses to be on their best behaviour
My choice is to opt for buttered or toasted? Either way the taste sensation's explosive!
Free range eggs and fluffy light batter coagulate in a bun designed to flatter
Aim for 'Currant' standards – always raisin', and you'll attain home-baking success that's truly amazing!
Before I finish it's imperative to trumpet, 'They're better than any piece of crumpet!'
But we don't want 'Mutiny at the Bun Tea' do we?
What a delicious alternative to bread, 'knead' any more be said?

POEM #13

Bringing home the bacon!

Have you ever seen trotters in fields, snouts in troughs, with pigs that never can seem to eat enough?
A summer barbecue is always an occasion to enjoy a sizzling bacon sensation
My local supermarket stocks shelves in my favour, with tasty bacon full of flavour
Unsmoked, smoked, middle or back – bacon is champion leader of the pack
Such mouth-watering bacon that's adored so much, sometimes my friend treats or else we "go Dutch"
It's the best cure for one's stomach when empty, afterall who can resist bacon butties a plenty?
The choice to cook, however, grilled, boiled or fried, is a constant dilemma that can't be denied
There's a foodie fun pleasure with every forkful, succulent, tender, lean and porkful
With outstanding freshness to the fore, just one taste and I insist on more!
Streaky, fat, salty, lean, my dinner plate is always clean
The opportunity for healthy feeding emanates from original country farm breeding
Mmmm! That inviting aroma as I awaken must be Sunday morning's rashers of bacon
It's fair to say rashers speak louder than words Speaking as an egg? I wouldn't scramble for anything less!

POEM #14
More Cheese...

Utterly delicious cheese always entices, especially when purchased at the keenest of prices
My favourite cheese competitively priced looks nutritious, delicious all ready to slice
Colourful and crammed with flavour, such desert delicacies are a food to savour
With a galaxy of cheese selection, mellow Edam receives the best reception.
This great 'all rounder' is tastefully surprising, whether grilled, grated, cubed or bought merely for slicing.
Always to me it's an alluring sight for beneath that red skin lies a delicious bite
It's creamy, smooth and full of taste, much too yummy to eat in haste!
From your local grocer the flavour's assured – fresh as the day it matured
When you're watching pounds and saving pence – the combination makes common sense
Whether on crusty bread or crispy crackers, Edam cheese makes happy snackers
Served in a hearty flan or with ham, it makes me dream of Amsterdam.
One can make exciting dishes, or just nibble it, if one wishes
Lunches, parties, dinners or picnics, Edam's the cheese with the vital statistics
It's tangy, red and round frame offers fewer calories per pound to gain
Undoubtedly this wedge has the edge in which to indulge without having to worry about the battle of the bulge

A creamy taste of pure delight, it is voted tops on party night
It has versatility and flair to discerning palates everywhere
On slicing freely with a knife, bread and crackers come to life!
The taste of Holland superbly represented means palates are pleased and pockets contented
"Reddy" wrapped it tastes divine – the label is Edam, the pleasure's all mine
Tickling my tonsils, curling my toes, this cheese excites wherever it goes
This happy squaw has been wholeheartedly captured by that captivating redskin!

POEM #15

Pass The Cheese Board!

Cheesed off with cheddar and red Leicester, I would like to indulge in a French cheese fiesta
French fromage in all shapes and sizes, ensures my cheeseboard is full of surprises
Different varieties for supper, lunch and dinner – each fromage français is a cross-channel winner
With quality, good value and selection, I've got my hands on foodie perfection
Flavours are unique, the range extensive, French cheese is the finest, yet reasonably inexpensive
Delightfully creamy, certain to please, nothing surpasses fine French cheese
From creation to presentation, each cheese gives you a taste sensation
True to French tradition their standards never waiver, first for value, first for flavour
Camembert tradition or creamy blue Brie, make a tasty addition to crackers for tea
I would consider French bread as naked you see, unless it is covered in Camembert or Brie
Au matin or déjeuner, they're cheeses for le Gourmet
Whether lunching early, or dining late, make time to explore culinary France on a plate
Comments from my guests are my just reward, forget the dessert and pass the cheese board!

POEM #16

Fancy A Crisp?

Crunch for crunch aren't crisps the perfect munch?
I occasionally enjoy a bowlful of pleasure from the local store I treasure
I am only minutes away from my treat for today
This afternoon's snack is a wondrous sight as I lick my lips and take a big bite
For a great hand held treat, crisps are so dainty and neat
The only issue is that once you're game for a bite, it takes strong resistance to avoid nibbling all night
Bags of flavour, no fuss, no mess, easily swallowed they pass the stress test
Bringing chuckles and screams of delight, everyone shouts 'It's party night'
These packages of excitement for those who are needy satisfy everyone's hunger pangs, no matter how greedy.

POEM #17

Potatoes Fit For A Queen

Queen Maris Pipers beheaded, King Edward gone –
thankfully Jersey Royals are still number one
Nine out of ten butters who expressed a preference chose
Jersey Royals as their point of reference
These buried treasures from Jersey's shores are well worth
trading chunky chips for
Local greens from British soils enjoy mixing with these classy
Royals
Jersey's 'Royal Earth Force' tastefully satisfies the loyal greens
on the ground
Nothing can soil their reputation; I don't have to question
their Royalties
A little simmer for this deeply flavoured food is suggested
when one opts for the spud that's 'Hoe, Sow Good!'
Every morsel is ready to savour in seasoned butter and
peppermint flavour
With presentation fit for a Queen, let's save our gracious
cuisine!

POEM #18

How Do You Like Your Morning Toast?

Traditionally more British than most I enjoy breakfast with morning toast
It's the only breakfast that's worthwhile combining taste, tradition, quality and style
Marmalade and butter we're agreed, makes a successful breakfast guaranteed
For breakfast pleasure, use your loaf, indulge yourself and have them both
Doubly delicious, doubly good, they'll help start the day like breakfast should
My friends would throw daily dramatics if breakfast didn't include these wonderful classics
Toast all golden or well done with the best of marmalade is so much fun
These old fashioned accompaniments on toast make rising for work a pleasure...almost!
I always set the alarm clock's ring in time for my share of citrus zing!
With an early tea and slice of toast, I get to enjoy this mealtime the most
Wakey, wakey, it's a good morning to YOU, delight in eating your breakfast whatever you do!

POEM #19

Conserve

Around the world 'conservationists' savour a taste in jam unique in flavour
Whenever you suffer a hunger attack it's a healthy convenient anytime snack
Wherever you are, whatever you do, one little jar will fortify you
Such delicious flavours, I'm besotted – each jar prepared is perfection potted
Excellent choice, super taste, guests arrive, the table's graced
Buttered bread is haute-cuisine with this fruity go-between
The Earth's crust never goes to waste when spread with this jam's tempting taste
'Berried' treasure, well preserved – it's home-made jam – so spread the word!
Deliciously fruity, additive-free, this jam reflects how conserves are meant to be
Ordinary jam is quite outclassed with this fruitful quality unsurpassed
Finest fruit, peak condition, gently preserved in the family tradition
My Nana's conserves are always desired – flavours jam packed, deliciously inspired
Thanks to a secret recipe of age old art, beyond comparison they stand apart
Preserving flavour not preservatives, these traditional conserves deserve superlatives
Outstandingly appetising, exquisite to savour, perfect colour, dazzling flavour

Wide variety, delectation guaranteed, jammed with quality, special indeed

Exploding with fruity zest, they are the berry best

I am well travelled and from here to Siam I declare there is no finer jam

Here great tastiness is unfurled – jam today, tomorrow the world!

POEM #20

Dough a Dear

From traditional white served in a Scottish town to Waikiki Beach ordered toasted and brown
Hot or cold, for luncheon or dinner, the Earl of Sandwich has created an absolute winner!
The variety of fillings in between makes bread and butter haute cuisine
Daily, hourly, at home, work, airport or station, the British sandwich fuels our nation
The Earl not only satisfied his appetite, 'butty' made history when he got this right
Bite for bite, it travels light, tasty fillings in both gluten and gluten free brown or white
If you use your loaf with sticky dough you can provide a whole meal for the family to go
Perhaps add a mix of seeds for added texture, you know what to do without a lecture
The sandwich is perfect for the dining table when you're not feeling your best at being cooking capable
Let the greatness of the sandwich's essence be the gift you give to your guests who are present.

POEM #21
Chocolate Temptation

A delicious tempting chocolate bubble bar like iced champagne and caviar makes us say 'It's OK Yaar'
Not creamy or flaky but airy and tasty a light combination from the bubble formation
The sweetest sensation without a doubt has bubbles bursting from inside out
It's not just the bubbles that make the bar a dream but the chocolate between that makes it supreme
It's an exquisite production of bubblicious seduction – removing the wrapper's the only obstruction!
Tear the wrapper, bite and be bold, unlock the bubbles of chocolate gold
Every surreptitious bite is a chocolate lover's delight – it's hard to believe the bubbles are so light
The chocolate velvety coating keeps the bubbles intact, when taking a bite they burst on impact
It is the researched process of aeration that breathes new life into this chocolate sensation
Delicious, dissolving bubbles so different from the rest prove unequivocally that 'hole' foods are best!
Try the lingering tongue-test prior to biting to make your experience more bite-exciting
As you start to chew and the bubbles are gone, can you believe the lovely chocolate taste still lingers on?
Like a melting pot of chocolate dreams, this experience is better than clotted cream
Biting succulent, airy bubbles is a treat not to ignore, my think bubble says more, more, more
With such a chocolate bubble bath of taste, you can be sure that there will be no waste

Breath-taking bubbly sensation – enjoyed to intoxication

Multi bubblo tastum delicio aroma supremo chocolatus magnifico

The only bar where pleasure doubles, as you burst the golden chocolate bubbles

Velvety percolated chocolate to eat indoors or al fresco goes down well with a little expresso

A bubbly sensation so meltingly sweet, don't deny yourself this worthwhile treat!

POEM #22

Wimbledon Wonders!

Serving quality championships since 1877, Wimbledon and tennis are a match made in heaven
For style and charisma no other can surpass, it's the only great tennis still played on grass
Terrific tennis, class players, venue a dream, plus Wimbledon's tradition –strawberries and cream
Singles and doubles whip up world wide support, all players dream of winning on Centre Court
World's greatest players, thrills and passion, Wimbledon fortnight ne'er goes out of fashion
Seeing Murray, Nadal and Federer too, is every tennis enthusiast's dream come true
A Wimbledon champion continuously hears tennis groupies raising loud cheers
Matches are sensational, excitement notorious, atmosphere electric, strawberries and cream glorious
The players excite, the spectators mingle, ace serves delight in games double or single
Singles or doubles both hold the Centre Court, for excitement, tradition and service to sport
The veterans play, McEnroe yells, the crowd's delirious, 'No strawberries and cream! You cannot be serious!'
Djokovic shouts, umpires overrule, but security guards keep everyone cool
Wimbledon is filled with jubilation; the crowd is quiet enabling players' concentration
Faultless service, ace location, loved by fans across the nation
World class tennis and splendid cream teas mean continual servings of true expertise

Unmatched standards help champions emerge, as on court upon screaming victory they surge
Champion venue, there's no catch; a day at the courts wins game, set and match
As far as I'm concerned when it comes to strawberries and cream at Wimbledon – one good serve deserves another!

POEM #23
Wine

Sun drenched grapes, straight from the vine, can produce a wine so astutely divine
Fragrant, delicate, with a distinctive nose, such an aroma is virtually impossible to capture in short prose
This superb vintage selection sets taste buds ablaze while extra richness earns tumultuous praise
Tasting this liquid sun gives such pleasure making every bottle quite a treasure
To the connoisseur the flavour, well that's its forte, has a body that's decidedly naughty
As a choice of drink without exception it would not disappoint in its perfection
It pampers the palate, mellows the mood, and complements almost any food
High standards with handsome care, such well matured reserves are so increasingly rare
Drinking a pleasure is never a duty when offered a natural wine that is fruity
Especially when these succulent grapes of great repute are converted into a champagne flute
No need to be fussy whether rose, white or red, tasting proves this liquor's well bred
Every bottle brings its guarantee – the ultimate nectar of consistency
Why don't you yield to grape temptation and pick up a brand new taste sensation?

Infused with pasta, cooked al dente, add vino, great
company – excellente!
It's classically aromatic, lively, and invigorating, never
insignificant and often leaves one contemplating
Good fruit, good nose, calm composure, quiet repose!

POEM #24

Ahhh! Butter

Ahhh! Butter is the love of my knife
It is borne of pastures green, a spreadable, edible go-between
It turns my little pepper seed cracker into a real lip quenching smacker
With more illusory, seductive powers than champagne, chocolates or garden flowers
It's a thorough' bread' spread that brightens up my daily bread
Delicious memories linger on long after my deli sandwich has gone
I consume it with an irresistible passion on Friday's frequent crumpet ration
How could it be spurned? Real butter is so perfectly churned
The taste once acquired is forever desired
As an indulgent, informal supper lust, it's the ideal choice for the upper crust!

POEM #25

Pâté Pots

Are you tired of scampi, caviar, squid? The answer may lie under this little pot's lid!
Tasty delicacies like this are unable to be resisted once these pot tops become untwisted
I consider that home-made pâté and paste are always deserving of extra cupboard space
Traditional skills honed with fine meat selection ensure handmade pâté can be made to perfection
Old fashioned recipes can't be beaten...best pâté ever eaten
Natural ingredients used are deliciously edible, easily spreadable and the value's incredible
In my personal opinion, the best-dressed bread wears a discerning individual pâté spread
It's so easy to turn the daily humdrum into an echo around the table of 'Yum-yum'
Furthermore, home-made pâté pots help me make ends 'meat'!

POEM #26

Grate Expectations

Feeling low, down on your knees? Pick yourself up with a wedge of cheese!
Crackers about it – never cheese-bored – its fatal attraction can't be ignored
With so many kinds – local and exotic – the power of cheese is undeniably hypnotic
Since childhood days when it was on ration, it has been my consuming passion
Love at first bite, Gouda to blue – their tasty tang will woo you too
I crumble at its seductive touch, grateful for the food I love so much
With every tasty, delicious bite, my epiglottis wiggles with delight
I'm crackers on cheese, when it's cheese on crackers!
An abundance of tastes from many nations complements my favourite appellations
With tasty flavours I'm besotted, since my local deli range I spotted
Approaching the counter with a sigh, I fervently hope they have tasters to try
My lips encounter a lingering lesson of provocative tastes from the delicatessen
Teasing my taste buds, melting my heart – I could wax lyrical, but where to start?
Home alone with my favourite wine – crackers and cheese, I'm on cloud nine!
From hard Cheddar to soft Philadelphia, cheese is calcium rich, what could be healthier?

Full piquant flavours are my passion, thanks to cheese delis they're always in fashion
Whenever I wonder what the Dickens to cook, I consult my 'grate' expectations cheese book
Whey hey, for the joy of a health-conscious mum, who gives guidance on protein and calcium
Heart melting heat, bubbling toast – a 'rarebit' of taste, cheese has the most!
To savour it fills me with elation, this source of sensory exaltation
Made by masters, matured by time, textures superb, results sublime
Grated, grilled, shaved or pied, tongues are most tastily occupied
The choice and quality at my local deli tempts and satisfies my discerning belly!
Don't rely on Cupid's dart serve heavenly cheese to win his heart
I crumble at the thought of Stilton's bite – 'grate' with wine, a connoisseur's delight
For meal variations cheese has it all, cheese and wine are my curtain call
Whatever my mood, whatever the weather, there are cheeses to please and to provide pleasure
The language of love being French, Italian or Latin, my heart melts on seeing a plate full 'au gratin'
Flavours abundant, choices galore, it may indeed be a fetish – but one I adore!

Following a romantic meal – cheese board arrives! Guess what follows? Contented sighs!

Palate pleaser, taste bud teaser, the way to his heart has never been easier!

Creamy, crumbly, sharp or mellow, it would melt the heart of any bedfellow

Going without would be diabolic – my passion has made me a cheesaholic!

I'm like a sailor – I love a different one with every port!

POEM #27

Nature's Way!

Those seductive hints of nut, fruit and spice, ferment my desire for food paradise
If nothing is added and nothing removed, can nature's harvests seriously be improved?
Eating organic has stopped the pain my friends have endured from a dreaded migraine
I love the organic guarantee – naturally nutritious and GM free
Deliciously wholesome, nutrient-rich and complete, for healthy living, you are what you eat
Into my lifestyle it perfectly blends, organic foods as nature intends
High quality food appeals to me which is additive and pesticide free
Guaranteed superior tastes from natural farming, nothing genetically modified to do any harming
Whatever your choice for fruit or veg, organic flavours have the edge
I savour the natural flavour without losing the taste under the influence of toxic chemical waste
What you get is what you C – wholesome ingredients, goodness naturally
They're healthful in so many ways without nasty artificial sprays
Expertly grown with tender care, ensures natural vitamins, beyond compare
While growers perfect them, the wise will select them
Protecting family wellness is so important so chemically grown food becomes less abundant

Mixing wholesome ingredients as nature intended means healthier families, well recommended
It's natural, healthy, preservative free everything my body should be
To befriend our planet we need to grow ORGANIC
Only Real Genuine And Natural Ingredients Count
My preference? I like eating with ease – not E's.

POEM #28

Pommes

Fertile orchards and sun-drenched trees – Isaac Newton would 'fall' for these!
Seasons come and seasons go but the taste of apples always grows
They mature at leisure and pip all others for peeling pleasure
'A' levels, Ooo levels, whatever the test, teacher knows that apples are best
Whatever colour or shade of skin, there's goodness, taste and crunch within
Crispy, crunchy, a splendid buy – looks to match – feast for the eye
Refreshing fruit, uplifting treat, natural goodness is not to be beat
One swallow seen improves my mood, complementing our picnic food
Orchard freshness revives memories past, dreams of childhood picnics last
A tantalising treat to drink or eat, juicily wholesome, temptingly sweet
Sipping liquid sunshine through a straw, couldn't please me any more
It reminds me of summer days, chilling out, catching some neutrino rays
Sparklingly fresh, delectably drinkable, any other juice would be unthinkable
Right through to the core, my senses shout more!
Quenches thirst best, leaves me h-apple-y refreshed.
Pommes are – Perfectly Outstanding Munchy Mouthfuls Ensuring Satisfaction.

POEM #29
Kitchen Mixer Sensations

With a 'blend' of innovation and 'eggspertise', my home baked cakes never fail to please!
I make my kitchen the place to be with great ingredients and technology
When using good ingredients one can trust, a reliable mixer is a must
Excellent results, design and precision make using my mixer an easy decision
A blend of great food and great recipes too – having this aid makes dream meals come true
It's not just a food processor, but a master of art, creating 'eggstravaganzas' for those in my heart
Quality ingredients mixed with care give me results I love to share
Following an old family tradition – the finest ingredients make for the best nutrition
Finer quality than off the peg – remember there are no E numbers in an egg!
Together with my free range imagination, I create culinary mixed sensations
Eggcellent results with a mixer aid, 'smashingly' tasty and perfectly made
Perfectly beaten, expertly blended, my food tastes divine, as nature intended
Creating cuisine that will always impress, all safely prepared with complete finesse
Chopping, blending, beating, slicing, whisking, shredding, mixing, dicing

My mixer achieves this vast selection, ensuring consistent baking perfection

I don't bake mistakes, just 'eggceedingly' good cakes!

Empty plates and a satisfied smile make home cooking worth the while!

Putting all my eggs in one gadget!

POEM #30
Liquid Pleasure

With a warm, rosy welcome, I need no persuasion,
Calvados and Normandy are the perfect liaison
Distinctive flavour is the Calvados tradition; there are no substitutes, so no competition
Calvados and Normandy are a 'spirited' pair so to sample their delights you must be there
Enchanting surroundings in which to discover, one sip of Calvados can soon lead to another!
Its warmth and character I adore, my favourite tipple I get to pour
In rustic Normandy, steeped in tradition, a rich tapestry of flavours comes to fruition
Food is delicious, brandy the best – I'd surrender to the Norman Conquest
The sweetest apples plus Gallic flair, gives a dash of panache – the savoir-faire
From rosy red apples to golden treasure, Calvados from Normandy is pure liquid pleasure
Sheer indulgence, so much to see, dreams fulfilled, so sweet – merci!
To savour the flavour in such a picturesque setting, embrace the unique experience as it's well worth getting
One part Normandy, two parts sun, stir in Calvados, pour out fun
Tasting sublime, perfection throughout, Calvados is something to write home about!

POEM #31

Organic Octaves!

Organic food on a product label suggests healthy food's always served on the table
Such nourishment is wholesome, natural and pure – traditional values that do well to endure
Naturally grown without genetic modification is much healthier and tastier in my estimation
Choosing organic is a guarantee for natural foods that are GM free
When pesticides are used our health is affected not to mention the wildlife which must be protected
Natural ingredients promote good health, better by far than possessions and wealth!
Soaked in sunshine, tended with care, nothing's more natural anywhere
Expertly grown with an eye on profusion ensures natural vitamins and no added confusion
Natural ways farmed give superior taste, nobody's harmed and there's little or no waste
Mixing wholesome ingredients as nature intended, means healthier recipes come recommended
Wholesome meals that are naturally organic provide natural goodness and a taste, fantastic!
Containing a wealth of health in every particle, there is no mistaking the genuine article
Organic flavours are superbly keener so let our children's future become much greener
There's nothing added and nothing removed because nature's best cannot be improved

Organic input gives us minerals and vits which rejuvenates our bodies' bits
A healthy diet every day helps to keep the doc at bay!

POEM #32

Sherry Delights!

Sherry provides mellow fortification for exploring Cyprus as a dream destination
It's smooth, rich taste and delightful sensations evoke thoughts of golden locations
Troodos Mountains to Mediterranean Sea; sherry and Cyprus thrill me
Chance of a lifetime, wonderful vacation, made more accessible with airline co-operation
Breathtaking sights, classical delights, with Cyprus days and sherry nights
Historical beauty sunshine galore, unlimited sherry who could want more?
From a passionate past, comes a sherry unsurpassed
As the Cypriot sunshine warms my skin, a glass of sherry warms it from within
Delicious drink, sunny isle, Sherry & Cyprus make me smile
Sensational beaches, water's perfection, drinking iced sherry – my Cyprus connection
Favourite tipple, dry or sweet, warming sun – my joy is complete
Spectacular, sun-baked beaches, scenic perfection, this is my idea of heaven
There's natural beauty, duty free, secluded coves and sparkling sea
Fabulous climate, traditional sherry, leaves me feeling quite merry
Long lasting sunshine and sherry supreme, clearly a clever connoisseur's dream
Cyprus climate can be very hot, but sherry, pale, dry or cream, hits the spot

Sipping sherry on Aphrodite's shores will have you coming back for more
Dry sun or pale moonlight, sherry in Cyprus is sweet paradise!
This cool delicious fortified sensation ensures a perfect memorable vacation
And the recipe for next year's holiday destination after much discussion and contemplation?
Will be dry weather, a little vino, medium tan and sweet memories sourced in Portofino!

POEM #33

Mmmmm! Coffee!

Coffee! Music! What can one say? Scrumptious way to start the day
Its mouth-watering aroma has to be right, awakening you punctually refreshed and bright
Gentle music and water warming means smooth tasting coffee every morning
Full-bodied flavour is so appealing when facing that Monday morning feeling
As you rise and shine with the sun in the East, the aroma's divine accompanied by breakfast or feast
At the dawn of the day it gets me up, dressed and away
It helps even the chronic sleepy head face the thought of leaving bed
A cupful taken early morning helps to stop persistent yawning
Delicious coffee right on cue with rich aroma filtering through
Arousing aroma, seductively blended, irresistibly filtered, and stylishly vended
Medium ground or filter fine it smells delicious, tastes divine
In chunky mug or fine bone china, this real coffee's flavour could not be finer
Freshly brewed coffee made the right way, filters my worries leaving me relaxed all day
I can always sip into something special as host, although coffee's the one that rules the roast
Tastefully enticed by rich aromas to savour, guests can enjoy a refined coffee flavour
Original, distinctive and classically blended, it ensures all occasions are perfectly ended

No fancy gimmicks or passing trends, just finest beans, perfected blends
The luxury that filters through brings the good life home to you
Deserving a wave of the chequered flag, a terrific blend has success in the bag
Every grain's a winner! I never spill the beans when it comes to haute cuisine!

POEM #34

Five Freedoms Part 1

Make healthy farms a fact, not fable! Buy healthy produce if you're able
The rearing of animals is extremely humane and buying these products ensures standards are maintained
Uncomfortable animals have no choice
Let your actions as buyer be your voice
High levels of welfare help animals thrive; they give better products, lead happier lives
Well-nourished and contented behaviour, the RSPCA are the farm animals' saviour
The RSPCA protect and respect animal freedom from neglect
Guaranteed goodness, fresh and tender, trusted suppliers – no contender
Best behaviour for man and beast assures quality care and food that's a treat
Pigs still wallow and hens still scratch, knowing they're raised on a Freedom patch
Hens can cluck and spread their wings, piglets root and dig for things
Perfectly produced with 'welfare' in mind, every Freedom Food is a gourmet's find
A conscience clear's worth an extra few pence, supporting this scheme simply makes common sense
Reared safely and healthily with freedom from pain; no cruelty to animals, only consumer gain
Treating animals fairly is as important to me as healthy eating is for my family
Buying other brands can be a lotto, respect for all animals is a healthy motto

When animal welfare passes every stringent test, the resulting products are definitely the best
Quality of life is a right for all; Freedom Foods protect animals great and small
We must take time to care, because it can be a cruel world out there
Farmers please keep in mind that we like those who are most kind
Remember sanity and wisdom in farming are not harming!

POEM #35

Five Freedoms Part 2

An animal's life can be tough and 'Old McDonald' doesn't do enough
The Freedom Food label tells me extra care has been given toward farm animal welfare
I believe in Freedom's Five, for all animals when alive
Freedom Food products are a guarantee, that mouth-watering mealtimes are cruelty free
Freedom from suffering, freedom from pain, freedom from food that is farmed with shame
Farm produced, reared as nature intended, is cruelty free and tastes simply splendid
Kindness and comfort, all cruelty removed, ensures a quality of product that cannot be improved
Freedom Food guarantees the highest standard invented, leaving both palates and animals contented
It's such a delight to contentedly eat the best cared for foods I could meat!
Food produced the Freedom way proves that care and welfare pay
Choosing the label is my guarantee, I am supporting a chain which is cruelty free
Producers are monitored, standards are high, this customer is confident to buy
I never have any reservation with the Freedom Food certification
An animal's need must come before human's greed!
When I choose to eat meat I really care that the RSPCA monitors animal welfare
Space, not confinement, dignity, not distress, food with Freedom at its best

The animal kingdom shares our earth, we must honour their freedom, respect their worth
Unrestrained animals are a pleasure to see, plus exceptional value – yes, that'll do me!
Stick to the Five Freedoms to the letter, your roast on Sunday will taste a lot better
'Cluck, Baa, Oink, Moo' when we're happy so are Ewe!

Section 2
Miscellany Moments

It gave me great pleasure these words to compile
I hope some make you laugh and many more make you smile
The poems are created at random from thoughts
Their intention to communicate hope, joy and love.

POEM #36

My Money Account

I need a safe haven for my hard earned 'dough!' for, alas, on trees money does not grow
When I first started saving as a local student, I opened an account to teach me to be prudent
Deutschmark, Dollar, Pound or Peseta, the calibre of service couldn't have been greater!
As I know the choice is up to me, I need an account offering flexibility
Accessibility, planned profitability, defines a bank of suitability
Have banks in recent years lost direction? Do they no longer guarantee financial protection?
Ten years ago in banking we did trust. An Instant Saver was a must
The discipline of a little saved each day would permit a balance of work and play
Their sterling performance an assured safe bet with all administration requirements allegedly met
Today the banks need to take a look before I'll accept their little cash book
I need to see my savings rise as I've come to expect interest as the prize
Creating greater wealth for me helps me to help others in deep poverty
Could our banks give a global guarantee that every transaction will be trouble free?
Revert to tradition of being safe and sound, hiring staff with a duty honour bound

Separate out plain banking divisions from those governed by algorithmic conditions
Courteous care with each transaction, offering a saving's home with complete satisfaction?

POEM #37

My Dream Kitchen

The space is free to create my dream
My brochure choice, "Inspiration" is the theme
Simple lines with refined taste,
Nothing left out, everything in its own place
With the latest style using curved doors,
My feet as I walk are on warm, wooden floors
The LED lighting creates accent light,
The range in the corner's a beautiful sight
When I look through the door and see my own baking
I know that my choice has been months in the making
No central island to distract;
A few wall units to create impact
A one and a half sink window-side for good measure
With matt black worktops, so cleaning's a pleasure
Appliances hidden, fresh flowers on a lit shelf,
Ah! At last time for tea and a cup to myself
So if you want a kitchen read this, be inspired
It could soon be your own team of men who are hired!

POEM #38

A Lady's View!

Embodying a unique blend of elegance and style
This quintessential grand tourer has the capability to beguile
With full unadulterated potential, luxury and interior mood lighting
This discerning lady's charisma to step in proves most inviting
With exquisite Crewe craftsmanship and striking innovative design
Every feature has been considered from the practical to the sublime
Clean superformed lines and a wide, low body evoke a sense of speed and presence
The Bentley Continental GT coupe is without doubt unmatched in its magnificence
With an outstanding performance delivering 900 Newton Metres Max Torque
The thrill of driving this beauty exceeds flying to New York!
The forty-eight valve Active Roll Control system senses road conditions
And instantaneously changes the car's movement to eliminate any handling inhibitions
On unlocking the car, my preferred pre-programmed sequence of exterior lighting is displayed
The physical experience of driving this tourer is truly as exhilarating as it is portrayed
At a top speed of three hundred and thirty three kilometres per hour
It's as fast as a Formula 1 racing car, demonstrating phenomenally supreme power

A six litre, twin-turbocharged W12 engine defines a step change in technology
Daily adventures across Mother Earth in this impressive vehicle will transform one's energetic physiology
The seats are minimalist in style with a streamlined design for ease
Smooth centre panels maximise the effectiveness of heating and massage functions, if you please!
Such exclusive, considered digital features and personalisation
Fully support my moods from passionate drive mode to one of calm contemplation
Electric steering improves feedback to the drive so that it always feels right
This gives me security and protected comfort over use both day and night
Can you believe I am able to backlight the treadplates in my chosen colour?
This is so exciting I can't wait to tell my mother!
I remember vividly my own jubilation when I took my first Bentley coupe drive trial
That was before the latest model with four driving modes accessible at the touch of a dial
Effortlessly efficient, emission levels are among the best in its class
The most advanced Continental ever including a sunroof of panoramic glass
Dual clutch transmission provides impressively quick

gearshifts and smooth acceleration to enhance the car's energetic character
As an exceptional birthday treat I have decided that this discerning lady will be my one indulgence hereafter!

POEM #39

India

The chance of seeing India by steam is truly a charwallah's dream
A moveable feast, exquisite cuisine provides a service fit for a queen
Posh and pampered all the way makes for a delightful holiday
Trained in luxury, 'coached' in style, imitating the 'Raj' mile after mile
Better than elephants, Maharajahs agree, travelling in style drinking Indian tea
It traces the passage of millions through the land of far pavilions
Memories of India sure to last, romance and mystery of the past
The splendour of the Maharajah's puffer spells magic to this railway buffer
From steamless age to ageless esteem, India's splendour expresses a dream
To enjoy such a break among palaces, shrines, demonstrates co-operation along the right lines
Palaces, culture and crafts to see; vintage India – my cup of tea
India's wooing, luxury viewing, senses renewing, the thrill of a lifetime ensuing
Adventure and palaces have much appeal with a view from a luxury train it's surreal
I am truly living the vision like a Raj as I continue travelling on my way to the Taj
This is unequivocally something to savour, a romantic journey with Eastern flavour,
Fulfilling an exotic dream transporting me under the power of steam.

POEM #40
The Conservatory

Healthy plants in a room with a view make a gardener's dream come blissfully true
A conservatory adds a new dimension, to lovely plants grown with care and attention
A combination of the two will make plants bloom the whole year through
This glass enclosure will speedily advance the blossoming of the most difficult of plants
Beautiful plants are grown with ease, thanks to shelter and horticultural expertise
It is the ultimate foundation, for a blooming population
A sunny, elegant, conservatory room shows off to advantage each beautiful bloom
This conservatory of great attraction can give hours of pleasure and complete satisfaction
These structures provide overall protection, transforming surroundings to pure perfection
Bright cosy housing, good food to eat, makes a houseplant's life wonderfully complete!
Clean and efficient, just granules of clay, it's wonderful growing plants the conservatory way
Come sun, rain, wind, heavy hail or snow, the house plants have plenty of 'get up and grow'
For a pedigree plantation displayed to perfection, a conservatory provides a first glass selection
Good shelter, light, moisture and feed, are the healthy way for them to succeed
Gorgeous greenery, flourishing flowers in a haven of peace to enjoy them for hours

Inspired by science, craftsmen built, they make plants flourish where others wilt
From orchids to jasmine the plants delight, in a paradise setting a cradle of light
Light, spaciousness and good foundations, give all the plants in-house good vibrations
Perfect soil and an ideal position, means the plants are always in tip top condition
In my potting shed lurked doom and gloom, but a conservatory makes everything bloom
Plants no longer browned off and neglected are revitalised now and specially protected
With colourful plants and a 'room with a view', make your own conservatory the envy of Kew!

POEM #41
Paris

For a Hyde bound lady who has De Gaulle to dream of winning, this Parisian encounter will send your mind spinning
Full of breathtaking delights spectacular sights, enchanting days and romantic nights
It's a must to say "UK adieu" for we are leaving for Paris à deux
Modern art, a peep at the past, gastronomic delights, we're packing fast
And having left our old pad behind, there are now more absorbing things in mind
There is so much more than an 'Eiffel' to see, with The Seine, Louvre and local patisserie
Paris is a lady of many charms, welcoming lovers with open arms
By day the beautiful historic sights, at night the romantic Paris lights
One part sightseeing, two parts shopping spree, stir in romance and voilà, pour out Paris
A taste for adventure, an air for fun, a delightful experience for anyone
With its spectacular sights, gastronomic delights, neon lights, make for evocative nights
Romantic, chic, with a special pzazz, the joie de vivre only Paris has
We climb the tower, sip champagne, dine at Maxims, then sail up the Seine
When sampling haute couture and haute cuisine, perfumes and pavement cafes complete the scene
Mind enlightening, romance brightening, pleasures uniting – so very inviting

Capital of love, vibrant sincere, puts spring in my heart
anytime of the year
Strange sounds, folks and sight, a thousand things to do by
morning noon and night
Romantic alluring enticing 'il y a toujours L'Elliscir de l'amour'
Like Dior – fun like Gaultier, romantic like Chanel, wicked
like Mugler – and always in vogue
Wining and dining, dancing chic to chic; would make a
weekend in Paris magnifique
Eiffel Tower – lots to view, fashion houses – dreams come
true, romantic dinners just we two
Chic, unique, 'bon appetite' for the fashion conscious lady a
fitting treat
This city cannot fail to hold you spellbound once a pot-
pourri of visual delights you have found
As if the Seine were sparkling champagne, each sight and
sound makes heads go round
With pavement cafes, vin ordinaire, taxis, bistros, girls with
flair, Paris is my love affair
Shopping, sightseeing, cafe-au-lait, then 'Joie-de-Vivre' at
the cabaret
Romantic, inviting with passions and fashions tempting –
delighting
By the time you see the Mona Lisa you'll know why she is
smiling
Perfect, Ambience, Romance, Interludes, Sensationelle!

POEM #42

The Humble Travellers Cheque

Always accepted whatever the land, a traveller gambles with cash in hand
Circumnavigation at a dash means cashing cheques not checking cash
Convenient, safe, impossible to abuse, take quantities with you, return the unused
Easily bought and simply cashed, lost or mislaid, they're replaced in a flash
Equal to gold, lighter to carry, accepted as cash, wherever you tarry
For minimum fuss and maximum speed, travellers' cheques are all you need
From street bazaars to the Sheraton, they're my global good Samaritan.
Pacific seas, Sahara sands, home or away, you're in safe hands
No matter what the local loot, these travel cheques will always suit
Many travel with hassle and stress, while wise men choose their book of cheques
Seasoned travellers know they pass the test, avert disaster and welcome success
Safer than currency, better than plastic, their worldwide acceptance is really fantastic
So well known in every land, only fools now go cash in hand
Stolen, mislaid, left at home, I've peace of mind wherever I roam
The service provided is simply divine, currency cheques and a useful helpline

Just a flourish of my pen, would produce Dollar, Baht or Yen
Security is their bottom line; it's where I counter sign
They are convenient, universally acceptable, totally dependable and above all very spendable
Secure, convenient, easy to use, the travelling companions I always choose
Their exchangeability is second to none, their world rating – number one
They ain't heavy, they're my cover!

POEM #43
Car Care

Superb lubrication and protective care gives higher performance and reduces wear
For maximum protection and minimum fuss, clean the car often and banish rust
One quick spray around the engine bay is all you need to save the day
You can drive motorway miles or inner city crawl, good car care is always on call
Make sure the car gets lubrication as this will help with moisture evasion
A lone lady driver need not panic, if her glove box conceals a liquid mechanic
Minor problems are soon made fit, by this worthy supplement to a car's tool kit
With a simple squirt one avoids disaster – anything squeaking or stuck is mastered!
Don't be driven to distraction, think rust-free, risk-free satisfaction!
As a motorist's must for car, truck or van forget St Christopher – and carry a can!
It can stay with you wherever you drive, so you can be sure you will always arrive!
It's the complete handy man in a neat handy can!
A spray a day keeps the AA at bay! A 'squirt' in time saves dialling '999'.

POEM #44

Lipstick on Broadway!

Like Broadway without a play, without lippy, my face would always look grey
Macy's fine store, Bloomingdale's best, with lipstick and make-up I'll outclass the rest
Whether dealing in nickels, dollars, pounds or pence, wearing my lipstick makes great fashion 'cents'
My cherry flavour lipstick – the sensual taste is immediately acquired, exquisite, seductive and forever desired
As an ordinary girl to Hollywood queen, eight hours later I am still living the dream
A twenty-four hour look that will 'keep' is ideal for the city that doesn't sleep
Alluring mascara to enchanting eyeline, I'd tower above every soaring skyline
Breakfast at Tiffany's, to Broadway at dawn, I'll look as terrific as Goldie Hawn!
Covering my flaws and enriching my pores, it gets the applause from 'Big Apple' stores
Each lipstick selected is such a star buy, each day feels to me like the fourth of July!
From Manhattan to Broadway, First Wives clamour, don't get mad – get lipstick glamour!
Take a stroll down Broadway looking fabulous, attracting admiring glances – miraculous!
I could take a bite out of the Big Apple and leave my mark!
I'd have the perfect enchantment, in this city of entrancement
Its appeal could get me more than a 'cor' in the Big Apple!

POEM #45

French Fashion

A beret – a hint of mystery, a dash of chic, a touch of France that's totally unique
A black velvet cape with deep folds full of swirls, when opened the beauty beneath unfurls
Designer lingerie looks truly divine, a 'special something' for anytime
French knickers, silky and saucy, seductive and sensual, perhaps I'll be naughty!
Black lace lingerie's wicked 'Seine-sation', match my cool, elegant sophistication
A Parisian ball gown that's stylish and sleek covers all that's provocative, classy, unique
A gown of black velvet with glints of pure gold, a suggested evening of secrets untold
Long black gloves, the height of fashion, arouse in me a dark sensual passion
Concealed with a pleasure to savour the scene, a treasure of beauty akin to a Queen
Silk stockings, so smooth, feeling fantastique giving an air of French mystique
My black velvet basque from a Paris boutique is suitably fitted and quite exquisite
A luxurious handbag designed by Chanel, black leather with clasp carved out of pearl
Stiletto shoes, the essential accessory, caress my feet out of bare necessity
My favourite perfume's smooth fragrance lingers from each hair on my head to the tips of my fingers

A Cartier bracelet in design so striking, pure luxury selected
to my own liking
My Parisian look is now complete, a style discerning
fashionistas seek.

POEM #46
Exotic Travel

Palm trees swaying and a drink so nice, it beats the UK with snow and ice
Oceans blue, palm trees green, this is a Caribbean dream
Sun kissed beaches, tropical breeze, long cool drinks and deep blue seas
With temperatures soaring and plenty of sun – more and more reasons to enjoy the fun
In bluest lagoons I catch my reflection, with my suntan oil ensuring total protection
Cool wine, sweet fruit – a tropical mix, the sea view has me completely transfixed
Wining and dining, beneath swaying palms, is so exotic shared with masculine charms
When fun and leisure come together, a handsome hunk completes the pleasure
Enjoyment here is beyond compare, there'd be no point in going elsewhere
Cool, refreshed, contented, tanned – a taste of paradise isn't 'half grand'!

POEM #47
Dental Crossing

Daily fluorides you can trust, you know careful action is a must
Preventative fluoride care beats a sitting in the dentist's chair
Take care to avoid tooth decay and brush up each day to show a faultless display
Take routine action, safe and sound, brush up, brush down and all around
Fewer dental drills and fills mean time for outdoor skills and thrills
Teeth clean proficiency is the game, dental safety is the aim
It's smile and be seen, start fresh and stay keen.
Think ahead to avoid neglect; follow the code and brush to protect
Without fillings, fresh and white, teeth so clean, shine at night
Put the brakes on tooth decay, by regular brushing every day
Know the value of protection, so teeth and gums will pass inspection
Your daily dentrification ensures fluorescent identification – one grin highlighting your peregrination!
Whatever your route or general direction, choosing fluorides will gain you protection
Remain alert to dangers dental and risks environmental
The operative word is 'prevention' so gums, like teeth, get regular attention
As dental problems disappear, mind and body are in top gear
While confident smiles make all aware, your dental care is beyond compare
By keenly aware, look ahead – choose routine care.

POEM #48
A Bug's Life

Tick-nology used for re-creation, Disney amuses my generation
Under feet, misunderstood, dreaming of heroes doing good
Always busy and in demand, always cool and in command
A wom'ants' work is never done
A working ant I'll always be, unless I win the lottery
Always caring, always fair, always loving and always there
Being little has many restrictions – bugged by parental afflictions
Worker ant the family's slave, appreciation's all I crave
Always jumping that's me, with the exuberant energy of a flea
Beetling along antennae twitching, for t'ant'alising food I'm always itching
Downtrodden with young bugs to feed, shopping's followed by a mobbing stampede
Being wee one has one major snag, avoiding feet becomes a real drag.
Birds keep bugging me 'cause I'm an 'ant'some guy
What a benefit it would be if I could fly
My brother's a pest and always bugging me
To the point where I've often had enough and wish he would flea
With my bug-infested home under constant attack, I am forced to turn hero to fight back
Everyday starts the same with me shouting, 'Earwig go again!'
Creeping, crawling achieving my aim, it's a hard life seeking fortune and fame
Yet, everyday I ant-icipate everything 'mite' one day be great!

POEM #49
Plants

Plants adore light airy homes with balanced nutrients for sturdy growth
Plants always thriving, always a sensation, in all ways a flourishing combination
Plants blooming like nature intended, can grow harmoniously when perfectly blended
Plants need nourishment and the right light, to ensure good results that will always delight
Plants nurtured in good soil you cannot surpass, and with regular feeding can win "best in class"
Plants guaranteed to thrive all year, when tended with constant loving care!
Of gracious living they deserve their share, good food, a pleasant home and loving care
Optimum conditions accorded, by beautiful houseplants rewarded
Outstanding grass mates with growing reputations, set the seal for excellence in flourishing locations
Quality, craftsmanship, style and technology, the key to success with an eye on ecology
Create a superb indoor garden with remarkable ease, with a little horticultural expertise
These genius gardeners have built their reputation, by putting quality and care into houseplant conservation
They're a natural partnership providing together, a plant person's paradise whatever the weather
They'd survive and thrive in their moist nutritious base, amidst light air and comfortable space
Satisfying their mineral appetite, controlling the temperature and light, create a great blooming site

Individually superb but together perfection, creating ideal conditions for my plant collection
For pedigree plants of outstanding vigour, a conservatory becomes de rigueur
Houseplants think they're in their spiritual heaven, and in such a stylish conservatory I would echo 'Amen!'

POEM #50

A Reality Check!

O mirror, mirror on the wall, that's not the person I recall!
The zipper strains, the waistband pinches, what can be done to reduce the inches?
With my ego punctured, my confidence deflated; if I was more streamlined I would be elated
A little past my sell by date, I need some help to rejuvenate
Having worked, wed, bred, and become somewhat jaded, would a spa weekend revive what has faded?
While relaxing, yet bracing, a wellness régime means good-bye depression and 'hello self-esteem!'
Such a wonderful stay in a stress-free zone would give me plenty of time for a body tone
As well as enjoying a complete overhaul, I could practice my favourite butterfly, backstroke and crawl
Being pampered to perfection, I would gladly look at my radiant reflection
No more fat tums and podgy thighs, only a healthy lifestyle regimen including exercise
So having accepted that I am not bionic, I give up my favourite gin and tonic
I indulge in a Crystal Steam Room treat at Stobo Castle's luxurious retreat
Opting for brie tart, fresh berries and celery sticks, there is no further need for a high glucose fix
Now happily facing the big 'five-o', I emerge refreshed and raring to go!

POEM #51

Welcome to the Wheel World!

Falcon flying mountain breeze, exercising wrist 'n' knees
Quick ascent up the mountain track, we saddle up with sandwich pack
Rosy cheeks and shapely hips come from healthy food and cycling trips
Bike riding can be extremely tiring unless on all cylinders you're firing
Given the chance peddle this treasure, feel satisfaction for mounting pleasure
A crucial cycle fun galore, fantastic cycling who needs more
Faster speed with care and grace, guaranteed a winning pace
When inner tubes suffer deflation, a lunchtime treat provides inspiration
Bikers, bakers, sandwich makers, know lunchtime treats delight all takers
Saddled with hunger, snack appeals, knapsack provides handy 'meals on wheels'
Saddle bags with lunch treat bulging, happy bikers soon indulging
With the leader of the pack, we're always exploring on the right track
Miles of flavour, success hailed, mountainous appetites newly scaled
Reaching heights and tastes supreme, rewards of working with a team
Though conquering mountains is very tiring, wholesome eating keeps our engines firing
We never 'tyre' of this selection, geared deliciously to perfection

Whether from traffic or urban decay, we respect the potential dangers on life's highway,
Time taken to preserve our bikes, enables longevity on our cycle hikes
All this exercise is sure to please, as we negotiate vistas and mountains with ease
We remember to take along a thirst quencher, geared for lovers of outdoor adventure
Whatever the journey or expedition, to summit up – spreads jubilation
Surpassing all other competition, we enjoy riding high in pole position.

POEM #52
The Boudoir Beckons!

It makes such good scents, when a little help you need in bedroom events!
For a body softly scented and silky smooth, your favourite fragrance is the one to choose
Softly, seductively, it sets senses reeling – a glamorous, amorous, million-dollar feeling
These alluring heavenly scents; seductive, sophisticated, subtly enhancing but never overstated
Splashed or sprinkled, smoothed or sprayed, this is how seductive dreams are made
Their fragrances cling alluringly to me – like being clad in luxurious lingerie
Smooth and sensual, fresh and light, they'll help romance on its way tonight
One application of perfume balm and my man will be captivated by my charm
Dressed in my pure silk lingerie, he'll whisper to me 'ma belle cherie'
Some women use men, Cleopatra used milk, for pure sensuality, I use perfume and silk
With glamorous foundations they gently enhance, guaranteeing many an admiring glance
Each is a silent but telling device, separately or together they always entice
Cocooned in such luxury, without a doubt, makes women feel good from the inside out
Containing everything pure and essential to my body they are fundamental
Their luxurious fragrance and sensuous feel were created to enhance the feminine ideal

Softly seductive, sensual too, let perfume and silk bring out the woman in you
Throw away P.Js, onesies and nighties and allow yourself feelings like Aphrodite
Perfume and silk are without a doubt, 'excellente' for every budding debutante!

POEM #53
Heartbeat of Your Soul

Deep within your soul, feel the core nature of your true being.
Feel a deep love within your heart for the you that you are living
In such dynamic changing global times be kind to yourself
And find a quiet space where you know you will be undisturbed in good health
Listen to your own heartbeat, the soul's gift of your unique expression
Reuniting you with the sound of Gaia as you close your eyes in mindful reflection
Breathe in the whispers of angelic realms and feel the ripples of truth
Of who you are and of your composed countenance of eternal youth
Your own unique heartbeat is your own living treasure!
Listen carefully to its rhythm and feel its sacredness in pleasure.
This is the energy of you at work, at sleep, at play,
Always throughout your physical existence in this lifetime on planet earth every day.
Know that when it is the right time for you, you alone have the power to release all pain,
Let go trauma, sorrow and grief to date in your life, never to be experienced again,
Safe in the knowledge that it is your birthright to love and to connect
With the divine spark that is your own life force of energy, in respect.

Forgive yourself for all thoughts, words and actions about which you feel you could have improved upon without distraction
Truly know that spirit sees you as perfect in your daily life to date.
You are living your own soul journey guided by Higher Self and your Innate.
You can choose to open your heart to a brand new beginning.
Be playful, act spontaneously and genuinely experience the joy of living
As a soul, this is indeed a magnificent time to be alive
To honour yourself, live life's mystery and to thrive
This is the lifetime that will make the difference.
For Mother Earth is blessed by your very existence!

POEM #54

My Tablet

Big on content, small in size, all the titles to tantalise
High tech accountants get executive stress while tablet book users have time to impress
A compact library with books supreme surely is a reader's dream?
Chapter, verse, sound and vision come to life with great precision
Fascinating reading, compact and neat – this novel idea has hardback books beat
Pocket classics in every sense, interesting, fun and for very few pence
Critics gave them rave reviews, every selection is headline news
Great value downloads full of laughter and tears, this tablet gives 'volumes' of pleasure each year
Hidden away from prying eyes, my sun-tan serves as the ultimate disguise,
Reading under a coconut tree, no one here will bother me
I relax in the sun as each dastardly crook, by the master of thrillers, is brought to book
The palm trees sway, the sun is hot and I've all day to follow the plot
It's a traveller's dream, by day or by night, an author supreme, and a reader's delight
From classic novels to popular fiction there is plenty of choice whatever your predilection
Racy romances or adventures and thrills, fiction or factual, a tablet fulfils
A download pack of famous fiction will overcome any space restriction

Stirring imagination and the ice in my glass I am lost in the spice of adventures with a touch of class

Whatever your age, what more would you need, sipping rum punch with a jolly good read?

Page by page, dreams I capture, time on my hands to start another chapter

Reclining on hot Caribbean sand, Le Carré's latest in my hand, deep blue sky matching sea – absolutely bliss to me!

Take it as read from an ardent book lover; you CAN judge a book by its tablet cover

Whether romance, mystery, horror or crime, one's mind is freed beyond reality and time

Be it leisure, pleasure, knowledge of the past, or laughter that you're after – the range is unsurpassed

For value and quality I have to concede, no-one can beat a good tablet to read

Jetting the world or working at home, so simple to use in any time zone

For a great name in reference, this reading choice is my preference

A tablet I am always recommending, this would be my 'happy ending'

Remember happiness is only a word away!

POEM #55

Consult the Dummy

I 'enter' and 'exit' without really knowing whether I'm actually coming or going
When megabytes meet micro brain a 'Dummies' guide can make it plain
When lost in jargon and each step's a bungle a Dummy book guides you through the computer jungle
From disc to tape, from bit to byte, a Dummies book will provide the light
Computing's explained as clearly as 'poss' for those who don't know their RAM from their DOS!
Consult the Dummy, press the keys, NOW I'm in charge with perfect ease.

POEM #56

A Bookworm

From Swallows & Amazons to the Philosopher's Stone, a
well-stocked library is a pleasure zone
An author's invention and reader's imagination are
interwoven threads that form a perfect combination
From thrillers to classics, fact or fiction, every book is my
addiction!
Personal computers may have a lead but they'll never
replace a relaxing read
From Animal Farm to Lady Chatterley's Lover, each is a
delight at the turn of the cover
Ancient or modern, heavy or light, each is a classic in its
own 'write'
From Amis to Woolf, from novel to verse, the library's
fabulous selection – but which one is first?
Books do more than educate, they stimulate, motivate and
liberate
With pages always open and easy to find, with facts
abundant, a favourite read makes other activities
redundant
They exercise my imagination and give my feet a rest; some
books even put my mind to the test
Thrilling adventures or a touch of class, books stir my
excitement when I've time to pass
Long hot summer, mind getting stale? Refresh your brain
with a classic tale
Favoured author or nom de plûme, whatever my mood,
books speak volumes

Books give so much laughter, many tears, and lots of love throughout the years
It's a 'novel' way to pass the time of day!
Yet, while books tell stories and photos last, the real experience is unsurpassed.

POEM #57
A Diamond Celebration

Have you ever pondered the beauty of a diamond with each flawless facet?
For as this delightful couple celebrate sixty years of marriage, their love everlasting is a priceless asset
This privileged marker of achievement spotlights the love that two people share
Throughout a lifetime filled with laughter, joy and wonderful experiences all wrapped up with care
I am sure on the Q.T. they both have some beautiful memories to cherish and treasure,
Of fortunate encounters which, like true love found, are too precious to measure
Allow me to remind you how these two beautiful souls first triggered a love connection
As inspired 'King Arthur' set to woo his beloved 'Maid Marion' with gallant deeds of amorous affection
Both keen enthusiasts for playing a game of squash in their local indoor sports complex
It's fair to say that this contemporary style of 'courting' left Patricia mildly bewildered and perplexed
But when Arthur proposed, Patricia's heart told her saying 'Yes' was right and true
If truth be told since the day they first met, she affirms she holds, 'Only eyes for you'
It was deemed appropriate that the newly wed bride of good judgement who had lived in Pollokshields
Post her wedding day would live in discerning 'new lands' of pristine houses surrounded by countryside and green fields
Both she and Arthur have been blessed with four children who have grown up with kindness and attitude

In Karen, Diane, Alan and John who treat their parents with love and gratitude
Now in more leisurely times, time invested is time well spent when Arthur is seated in front of the box
Provided the coverage features the latest golf and/or prices of shares and stocks
How wonderful to relax with the FT newspaper and a bottle of wine decided on a whim
While Patricia sits contentedly nearby with a recently poured glass of her favourite gin!
Ageless, timeless and debonair, the charm of love permeates everywhere
As you enjoy each new day in good health and continue to live life with ease and grace
May your love, friendship and fun endure across the ripples of time and space
For this amazing couple sharing success, prosperity and happiness, in peroration,
Let's raise our hearts and glasses to Patricia and Arthur applauding their 60th Wedding Anniversary celebration!

POEM #58

Garden Sense

A butterfly beauty softly emerging symbolising beginnings new, spreading world-wide happiness in colourful hue;
A cottage garden full of scent, pots of colour, time well spent
Colourful borders, grass so green, create an ever restful scene
Fragrant flowers, never ending, water feature stream descending, major pleasure – minor tending
Visually stunning, unrivalled ground, colourful, fragrant, paradise found!
Bright with flowers and shady trees, home to butterflies and honey bees
A wildflower garden is my dream, with natural simplicity as its theme
Heavenly fragrance, simply splendid, where everything grows as nature intended
Water feature, lawn, tree, shrubs, butterflies and blooms in tubs
Orchard, summer-house, woodland stream, room to wander, relax and dream
An ever changing display at its best, of flowers, fountains and statuettes
Tropical palms form this creation; spectacular, a subtly scented sensation
Fragrant flowerbeds, shady shrubs, patio with palms and no nasty grubs
Vibrant, exotic, exciting to see, joyful, relaxing and maintenance free!

POEM #59

Bath-time Fun

Bathroom lessons best taught young are happily practised when they're fun
Wash time fun, no tears or troubles, children love the power of instant bubbles
Everyone can safely play when dirt and germs are washed away
Gentle cleaning, making mess, bath-time washing, real success!

POEM #60
Laundry Quips

For minimal cost use pocket-size packs as these contain secrets others lack
Convenient and quick with results that impress, why would you gamble with anything less?
Their brightening and whitening's guaranteed, giving perfect results with expert ease
At 40 degrees, the perfect solution, a twenty-first century wash revolution
One small packet in your washing machine makes a big wash brilliantly fresh and clean
It takes wash and clean to a standard unseen that is eco friendly and going green
The cleaning agent is quite phenomenal with effective performance that is so economical
Only when water and powder combine, can you wave goodbye to grease and grime
Make carefree laundering a class act, and remember to use your powder power-pack
When your washing reputation's on the line, they'll keep it spotless every time
They never whitewash, just wash white!

POEM #61

Waxing Lyrical

Film forming over shine? Windscreens looking duller? Let wax move in to uplift jaded colour
From a choice of car products that will be protective, wax based items have proved most effective
Goodbye Mr. Chips, goodbye Mr. Scratches, help is here from the King of Waxes
For a super film buff, a star-spangled sheen, wax is easy to use for an outcome supreme
Cleaning, polishing, protecting too, a treatment of wax keeps cars looking new
Bodywork corrosion is kept at bay, preventing tomorrow's problem today
Results on paintwork are fantastic, built up grime disappears like magic
For phenomenal gloss and grime removal, it comes with its very own seal of approval
It's a car's own wardrobe of "coat-couture", a must for every lady's caring chauffeur!
For minimum effort, wax gives maximum shine, great protection from grease and grime
Its reputation is well deserved, keeping my car well preserved
I treat my car's paintwork as I would my own skin – with care and quality products to win
With a lasting shine every time, it's hello Mr Sparkle, Goodbye Mr Grime!
On motorway miles or city crawl, a quality wax protects overall
Shining your car too can be just a doddle, when you remember to cover your topless model!

POEM #62
Candid Camera

Bright crisp pictures snapped with ease, give us fun and memories.
Whether you are a pro or beginner, each camera click can provide a winner
For boys and girls grow up so fast, a camera ensures our memories last
Digital and compact, designed with skill, each photo shoot is one to thrill
Happy moments are captured forever, with plenty of family photos to treasure
Thanks to the camera's auto focus action, I obtain first class film speed reaction
With a high pixel lens, quality will never diminish – it will always win in a photo finish
There's nothing negative about photos approved, my views will be scene but clearly improved
Snapping shots from Preston to Portofino, I am an apprentice Mario Testino!
My cherished memories become works of art as my camera plays its supporting part
Using my camera is no snap decision, finest photos with perfect precision
Moments of life's celebrations and laughter, scenic perfection to peruse ever after
'Panoramic' hols or 'snapping' baby, I could 'develop' into a 'flash' lady
Focusing is quick, exposure is slick, perfect pictures whenever I click
My camera is the bridge between present and past providing 'Prints Charming' here at last!

POEM #63
Cups of Delight

Pretty or sporty, perfectly pleasing, lacy or naughty, tantalisingly teasing
The choice of collection proves enticing with beautiful bras at affordable pricing
An uplifting experience has been born, keeping abreast of fashion form
Imperfect figure, uncomfortably flat, don't worry there's a bra that can change all that
For personal style in a brand I can trust, I get rising inflation without going bust
For those with a figure voluptuously pronounced, cheques are not the only things that don't bounce
All on display 'shape' up to provide garments of beauty sold with pride
When shape and comfort are put to the test, there's no doubt these "cups of delight" figure best
Correct support, phenomenal style, reliable and comfortable mile after mile
They're flattering, fashionable and appeal to me. I feel the difference others see
Quality and value hallmark production, guarantee moments of romantic seduction
Blissfully comfortable, uplifting by-line, make your profile better than Manhattan's skyline.

POEM #64

Oils Well!

My little oil can exceeds DIY expectation as a top performer with impeccable reputation
Sprinkle, sprinkle little tin, it's my home's 'wonder medicine'
Infinite uses, value supreme, makes everything work like a Hollywood dream
Its perfect performance steals the show in office, home or studio
Manufactured with expertise, my little oil can lubricates with ease
It's not just a lubrican't – but a lubrican
Squeaks and problems large and small, my little oil can cures them all
Its reputation is renowned, its versatility will dumbfound
Multi-talented, highly rated, it solves problems that life's created
Its superb quality, protective care, gives star performance and reduces wear
Whatever the drama, complex or routine, my little oil can's always saving the scene
It's winning formula and universal action is paramount for complete satisfaction
For doors that squeak and jam, it's versatility in a can
Stiff hinges are foiled when you get them well oiled
Oil be freeing you in all the old familiar places
Just a couple of squirts and everything works
It liberates and lubricates from moving parts to garden gates
For smooth performance and control, it wins 'cans' down in every role

It frees locks and hinges from their rusting restraint, with action shots that give no complaint
My little oil can eases life's irritations, in an amazing variety of situations
Upstairs, downstairs, inside, out – my little oil can sorts things out
There's always an outstanding performance in the can
Oils well that mends well!

POEM #65
Christmas Chatter

Hark my mobile's gentle ring heralds calls for answering;
No cord to restrict my ambulation makes for further conversation
Upstairs, downstairs, front or back, I'm free to Yakkity-Yak
Although my family lives far away, it's cheap to phone on Christmas day
Never moving from the chair; press a button, calls right there
Grandchildren dialling Christmas cheer; the miles between us disappear
Telephones ring – are you listening? O'er the world – faces glistening
Beautiful sound – beaming around, talking in an instant wonderland
Anywhere worldwide – Glasgow to Perth, phone services prove their optimum worth
Christmas finds me reminiscing; family friends that I am missing;
If you can't be with those who matter, at least you can have a festive chatter
Ringing long distance makes the heart grow 'phone-der'
Seconds later I'm in touch; now the hurt's not hurting much
Oh what joy to me it brings when I hear five golden rings
Ding Dong merrily on high – it's heaven the bells are ringing
There's goodwill all along the line from Christmas Eve to Auld Lang Syne
When Gold is expensive, Frankincense sold out and Myrrh not stocked,
Wise Men give someone special a ring for Christmas!

POEM #66

What a Great Kick!

Champion performers, grandstand view, hassle nil enjoyment two
Crowds for the game are divided in cheer, but at half-time the fans are united in beer
Whetting the whistle with thrilling action, they guarantee cheering satisfaction
Pints a pouring; strikers scoring has every fan's excitement soaring
The players create a real sensation, for some its tears, for others elation
Raised in triumph, downed in defeat, a pint of beer hits the mark with thirst beat
Beer and football team up to score, a match made in heaven that has fans wanting more
Together they both have a taste of success that leaves their admirers feeling their best
They're both enjoyed with pride and passion and score instant satisfaction
Champion performers representing the thistle, offer plenty cheer at the final whistle.

POEM #67
Travel Break

Home or abroad, day or night, what is the secret to a quality life?
Putting aside the computer, phone and fax, I've decided to swim, sunbathe and relax
Over the clouds, far away, I've holiday insurance for every day
Tropical island, pure white sand, dancing by moonlight to the calypso band
With crystal seas and beaches divine, beautiful memories will always be mine
A carefree holiday lounging around in the magical Maldives, my paradise found
Swimming with dolphins, confident and free, what a pity I have only seen it on travel TV!

POEM #68

Aquatic Adventures

Mermaids, dolphins, treasures to see, amazing excitement under the sea
For ancient artefacts we all thirst, discovering secrets, being first
Romantic quest, mysterious venture, every child's dream of a tale of adventure
Fathoming out forgotten sights, surveying a world of sub aqua delights
Hidden treasures, surprises galore can be yours too, when you explore
Forgotten word, pleasures untold, beneath the ocean adventures unfold
Mythical city, Atlantean race, like the Ladybee- sunk without trace
Does Atlantis really exist? This is a riddle I cannot resist
Water way to fathom out what this legend is about
It's exciting beneath the deep blue sea – magical, mystical, beautiful and free
Manatees, coral, catfish too, it has the makings of an aquatic zoo
No shortage of content for divers' imaginations, this underwater world spans generations
Hidden lands beneath the sea, decode incredible mysteries for me
More knowledge of ancient civilisations can only benefit future generations
Fabled city charting mystical creation provides ultimate challenge and deep elation
History, mystery, second to none, a concentration of aqua fun
To be precise it sounds Nautilus but nice!

POEM #69

Motor-vation!

To be in tune, you have to be slick. My engine oil is the perfect trick
It's sumptuous quality, champion choice, friction's challenged, engines rejoice
Whether for engine endurance or cleaner emission, my engine oil takes pole position
It fully protects, is completely synthetic, pour it in and just forget it
Performance and protection's finest aid takes motoring into another decade
It makes science-'friction' a thing of the past continually proving it's up to the task
Friction lessens, speed increases, performance improves, wearing ceases
Its formula has three-way perfection: quality, performance and protection
Superb quality, protective care, ensures higher performance, reducing wear
Decades of research, knowledge so vast, gives 'oil'mighty protection unsurpassed
It lubes all the tubes of every facet, to allow you to care for your major asset
Spotless engine, minimum drag, my engine oil takes the chequered flag
It's undoubtedly the best insurance to promote esteemed engine endurance
This oil selection is one of distinction – that is a fact not friction

Motorway mayhem, city queue, designed for tomorrow,
keeps engines like new
With improved viscosity comes accelerated velocity.
Its protective lubrication, gives engines extra motor-vation!
Synthetic result of creative skill is Engine Oil 1: Friction 0.
Just go with the flow!

POEM #70

A Regal Baby Wish

Helicopters for dad, diamonds for mum, while the regal baby's wish is for a comfortable bum
He's sitting pretty well-protected, knowing nappies have now been perfected
A gurgling baby, a first class nappy is safest for Ma'am to keep her great grandson happy
With trendy gear, looking chic, he definitely does not want to risk a leak
No nasty leaks, no painful botty, they'll keep him dry pre the Royal potty!
Made to measure, soft to wear, "street cred" style for his derriere!
With stretchy comfort and fit just right, Royal baby's approval is watertight
Containing that tinkle when he toddles, so no worries about his wiggle when he waddles
The quality's unbeatable, fit is just fine – that's what counts on the bottom line
Snug, cosy, no leaks or puddles, happy Royal baby without nappy rash troubles
They're comfy, economical, skin stays dry, as for nappy rash tears, just wave bye bye!
Comfort matters! His "HRH Dryness" is best! Does your baby's nappy pass the bottom line test?
Bottom line, the perfect nappy keeps baby absorbed and mum and dad happy
Let your baby's nappies be your knights in shining pyjamas
The perfect nappy minds his pees and poos and comforts him so he can snooze!

Even my brave little soldier needs nappy care for his privates!
As we say in Scotland, his "wee" stories always have a 'nappy' ending!

POEM #71
Light Brigade

I am an advocate of greater energy efficiency and improving re-cycling proficiency
If you ask me where I get my thrills, I prefer mountain bikes to mounting bills
Long life cycles, geared to please, help me ride the energy squeeze!
Electricity consumption is kept at bay, preventing tomorrow's high bills today
Saving energy, saving pence, environmentally friendly, makes common sense
Energy saving bulbs, the ful'filament' of a dream, electricity bills to make me 'beam'!
From manufacture to ignition, they aid conservation and reduce emission!
Clearly made with sparkling precision, optimum optics give economising vision
'Bright sparks' formula for efficiency – 'less C02, less electricity'
Whilst committed to halting greenhouse crisis, pleasant shocks come from lower energy prices
I made the switch and got it right, less power, more light
Smaller bills are 'currently' paid – by the 'charge' of this 'light' brigade
Energy saving works like a dream – white in colour yet totally 'green'
They are 'current'ly the best h'ohm's -'element'ary my dear 'watt'son!
Their technology protects our ecology – making it the greatest glow on earth
They let me see my home in a whole new light!

POEM #72
Concorde R.I.P.

I had only one remaining ambition – to fly on Concorde and break with tradition
Fast as a bullet, the king of birds, to live my dream I was lost for words
Rat race victim of the daily grind, my VIP trip was a chance to unwind!
I was wilting, tired and weary of work, lunch on Concorde – what a perk!
This mighty bird stole my heart away, for a few short hours I could rest and play
Nothing could be finer than to fly the Concorde diner!
Its exciting new image was inspirational, high flying Concorde was just sensational
Its metamorphic transformation offered supersonic exhilaration
It was refreshingly cool, stunningly chic, the interior design of a style quite unique
Refreshingly different, 'the travel of tomorrow', Concorde set standards others could not follow
There were no fines to pay for speeding on this 'highway'!
For connoisseurs of taste and place, it made the perfect meeting space
I felt like 'Sir-Loin' of the ruling jet set, when first my eyes with Concorde met
Heavenly flight, lunch symbolic, a soaring success, it was just the tonic
Books tell stories, photos last, but the real experience was unsurpassed
By air to Paris in Concorde was divine! This time of my life was truly sublime

The shape of 'wings' to come – unfurled, my Concorde flight was outer this world
A taste of the good life from take-off to landing on a 'higher plane' that left others standing
Concorde's supersonic aviation pledge gave flying Mach 2 that extra edge
A droop nose feature could be lowered and raised, a technical marvel for which it was praised
Concorde was the 'flagship' of the aircraft fleet – elegant, luxurious, graceful and élite
Granted special permission to fly at low altitude was a testament to engineering gratitude
But, when Airbus refused vital on-going support, its future airworthiness was immediately cut short
An iconic fleet that was forced to be grounded left the public confused and rather dumbfounded
In commercial service for 27 years, Concorde's fondly remembered with much love and tears
Eiffel for Concorde as soon as I'd Seine it
It came – I saw – it 'Concorde' my heart!

POEM #73
Papworth Praise

As the driving force behind innovation
Of major heart and lung transplantation
We are gathered this evening for a very good cause
And for this I would ask you to give your applause
To Diane and Karen for their tireless preparation
Of encouraging you to make a heartfelt donation
Towards this renowned charitable organisation
Giving people life by performing breakthrough operations

The hope that is given behind every penny
Accumulates day by day to give many
A chance of a new life filled with inspiration
To create new happiness and gratification
To every member of Papworth staff
For their dedication and committed graft
Know that this is appreciated from the core of each heart
The gift of life – offering each patient a fresh start!
Thank you!
THANK you!
Thank YOU!

POEM #74
The Measure of Tapes!

Do you remember the days of tapes that gave us sound and dream escapes?
Beautiful colour, delightful sensations evoking thoughts of surreal locations
For sound and vision with German precision BASF was the logical decision
Each product delivered was built to last and perfectly processed to preserve the past
The image was clear, projection ideal, in capturing life – real to reel
The fine sound and vision generated suggested other brand tapes were second rated
Be it Walkman, hi-fi or stereo in the car, BASF tapes were the best by far
Other tapes soon faded and blurred, but with BASF this never occurred
Classical, pop, quality abounds, jazz, rock just listen to 'demo' sounds
The colour and vision reigned supreme with this brand in my video machine
Less distortion at higher volume drowned out my brother in the next bedroom
Whether Documentaries, Shockumentaries, Comedies or a Big Fight, BASF had the copyright
From faintest whisper to loudest roar, BASF tapes clearly captured more
Football, rugby, tennis or cricket, whichever sport who would want to miss it?
Their magnetic attraction guaranteed satisfaction superbly recording the dynamic action

Pavarotti's quavers never wavered; Madonna's shrieks were never weak. This was a product with sounds unique
Either watching Cilla or rocking to Queen, BASF tape recordings played back like a dream
They were appreciated by all types of winners, giving expert results for pros and beginners
With sound so sleek and unsurpassed, they were unique and not "tapecast"
For spoken word and musical note, BASF always had my vote!

POEM #75
Precious Moment

What you think creates your vision
Step outside, switch off your television
Important news will always reach you
Feel the freedom love can teach you
Wear silk stockings with suspenders,
Stiletto heels will be remembered
Take that walk forever promised
Smell the flowers of the forest
Know this time's a precious moment
That will pass like the tides across the Solent
Take the pressure off yourself
Leave your worries on the shelf
Throw your shoes off, feel the grass
It's time to live before you pass
Breathe the air, don't despair.
Know that someone's there to care
Whether it's a higher being looking at you from the ceiling
To some it may just be a feeling
Go with what is most appealing

POEM #76

Come Ride With Me!

Another Day Another Dollar
Loose your shirt, unbutton collar
Throw your coat aside, welcome to the ride…of your life
Come away with me
A whole new world to see
Fill your eyes with glee
Join the ride
I will be your guide
Welcome in the night
Whet your appetite
Come ride with me
You can only come
If you are up for fun
The journey's never done
When you succumb and ride with me
Come ride with me
Come ride with me
Let dreams expand
As hand in hand
I'll take you to a far off land
Remember leisure
Remember pleasure
Sun-kissed to perfection
Look at your reflection
Come ride with me.

POEM #77

Love to Love

Love to love
The pouring rain
Love to love
Being home again

Love to love
Your lover's kisses
Hug'n stuff
And gourmet dishes

Love to love
The sexual connection
Love to love
With all affection

Love to love
Annoying habits
Squeezing toothpaste
Feeling crabbit

Love to love
His heart, his mind
Love to love
His being kind

Love to love
That you are deserving
Love to love
That you are worthy

Love to love
His stroke of leg
Tousled hair
His touch in bed

Love to love
Each bird that flies
Love to love
Each baby's cries

Love to love
The soul that is YOU
And be content
With being true!

POEM #78
The Supervet

I love watching The Supervet
Fitzpatrick Referrals care about your pet
Each Visitor's treated as a VIP
Contributing to veterinary history

Supervet, Supervet
When you still have hope, he'll examine your pet
Supervet, Supervet
Noel and his team do their best for your pet

You'd wonder how each pet survives
Under the vet's precision knives
He engineers repairs to limbs
Applying screws and metal trims

Supervet, Supervet
When you still have hope, phone "The Bionic Vet"
Supervet, Supervet
Noel and his team do their best for your pet

He's without doubt a pioneer
A superhuman engineer
Protecting animals great and small
And lives in hope we'll love them all

Tiger, Otis, Scooby, Pixie,
Jasper, Lolli, Rufus, Dixie
Anja, Dolly, Mojo, Jake
We never tire of seeing the difference you make!

Supervet, Supervet
On animal welfare, we're not there yet!
Supervet, Supervet
Let's spread hope and love for each hard-to-cure pet

If this inspires you on why animals matter
Then #FollowTheLove @KOKOChatter

POEM #79
Remembrance

What a lovely idea to celebrate peace
With a new time-honoured show of a white poppy wreath
Why would you not want to step up in your maturity
And honour ALL fallen souls, with grace, in unity?
To war, as in physics, there must be a pair
The enemy and an opposing regime must be there
In storytelling of war, victors proudly take their salutes
While heroic tales of their enemies they'll often rebuke

Red poppies, white poppies, let's respect the past and forgive
Now we are creating a new earth of peace in which we can thrive and live

It's time to wake up to the illusion of duality
And face up to the truth of your own multi-dimensional reality
When the 'I' fights with another, that 'other' is me
Open your heart up to love; allow your vision to truthfully 'see'
The significance of red poppies will always have their place
But with the passing of time there is now enhanced data to embrace

Red poppies, white poppies, let's give ourselves the gift to forgive
Now we are creating a new earth of peace in which we can thrive and live

The red poppy's a symbol of passion and groundedness in defence
The white poppy symbolises purity and peace without pretence
We are in a unique, earth revolution, the evolution of humanity
Feel the love deep within your heart and take charge of your sanity
When you can stand in your power and let go judgement of another
You will learn to love ALL souls as if they were each your brother

Red poppies, white poppies, we set ourselves free when we can forgive
Now we are creating a new earth of peace in which we can thrive and live

Remember your ancestors' actions with honour and love
And celebrate the potential of heaven on earth, as above
No-one is superior or inferior to another as goes the lesson of healing
So step up in your thinking and connect with your feelings.
Any pain, grief or guilt that remains suppressed
Will destroy your chance of inner happiness
Let's put aside differences and become an 'imagine' world nation
Living lives filled with fun, joy, laughter and innovative creation
Respect the past for in the remembrance comes the light
Step into your wisdom and be grateful for the wonder of life.

POEM #80

Tree View

The trees stand still, each with their story
Summer is here and they're laden in glory
In all shapes and sizes, they vie for position
Their roots lay foundations without inhibition
The chestnut, the oak, the ash and the elm
Can all play hard ball and stand their ground well
And each with its own pace of growth and leaf texture
Makes the surprise of each view a real pleasure!

POEM #81

Kiss

You're a face in a crowd, will you please turn around
And kiss me?
Once you step off the train I might not see you again
And you'll miss me
Your attractive, you're fun, keen to meet someone
Come and kiss me
Get up from your seat, come on over and meet
ME!
Let me see your face smile, let your humour beguile
ME!
Your sexy, you're fun, keen to meet someone
Come and kiss me
Your looks are so cool
You are nobody's fool
You have just made me drool...
Now that you've finally kissed me!

POEM #82

Path to Happiness

How many 'likes' do you have on your phone, loads of
'virtual friends' but do you go home alone?
Go get on a train, try a taste of adventure, talk to the
passengers about life, love and architecture
Mention how you would like to rule the world,
Reduce taxes, save the children, leave no stone unturned
Tell a joke, have a laugh, learn a new trick
Take a leaf from Stephen and write your bucket list...quick!
Know that every breath you take is a gift
Use it wisely, stay true to yourself and don't drift
Away from your goals and desires in your heart
Let friends old and new play their part
In helping you seek contentedness
When all the rest are hyped with stress
If you're not having fun, it's not worth doing
So go with your gut, don't get stuck in a rut
Walk the path to happiness!

POEM #83
Confidently Cool!

Be cool
Stay cool
Don't be a fool!

If you said I was normal, they'd say I was hormonal
Who defines normal? And what does it matter?
Be yourself, ignore idle chatter!

Be cool
Stay cool
Don't be a fool!

If you're earth shatteringly good, there's no need to be rude
Just say it as it is
Be yourself
And don't get into a fluster!
Instead your inner confidence muster!

POEM #84
Base Note Oils

Aromatherapy base note oils to which you can refer
Are Ylang Ylang, Sandalwood, Parsley, Myrrh
Aniseed, Benzoin, Cinnamon, Clove,
Cypress, Fennel, Frankincense, Rose,
Black Pepper, Nutmeg, Ginger, Neroli,
Cardamom, Cedarwood, Jasmine and Patchouli

Let cinnamon's spicy massage oil leave you in warming mood
While jasmine's floral fragrance has you energised and feeling good
A massage with black pepper is great to conquer muscle spasm
Ginger compress is comforting and can fill a healing chasm
Clove skin care helps with respiratory infection
Bath time with frankincense delivers calming reflection

Aniseed produces a relaxing feeling aiding flatulence and indigestion
Sandalwood as a cream compress is soothing for insomnia protection
The woody scent of benzoin treats throat infections and skin irritations
Fennel skin care energises one's body and can also be taken via inhalation
Patchouli used in massage is best for damaged skin
Exotic ylang ylang is brilliant to avoid stress setting in

Menstrual disorders are helped by inhaling smoky myrrh
A soothing cedar wood massage eases eczema and acne that occur
Parsley refreshes one's emotions and can stimulate circulation
Fresh cypress oil is a natural disinfectant, eases digestion and wonderful for rejuvenation
Spicy nutmeg oil has warming properties good for tired muscles
Rich, floral neroli inhaled may leave you with euphoric corpuscles!

Cardamom oil treats rheumatic aches and arthritis well
While the delicate sweet, rose oil is uplifting just by its smell.
These base note oils are a quick aromatherapy checklist
To which you can add your own oils that I may have missed!
Thank you kindly for paying attention
Now enjoy heaps of fun mixing your own oil inventions!

POEM #85

Spa Treat

Formerly frumpy, fat and forty – we're faithful friends – now slim and sporty
Under this body of forty two, there is a supermodel breaking through
A day at the spa was his proposal for dealing with my waist disposal
No deadlines, targets, phones or fax – trimmed, slimmed and pampered – let's simply relax
He works too hard and needs a break, to change from lard back to prime beefcake!
I work out with multiplied vigour, change vital statistics and round down my figure
Now I've successfully trimmed my thighs, they only need some massage and gentle exercise
Relaxing yet bracing, a healthcare regime, means good-bye depression, hello self-esteem
When waging war on cellulite, a local spa break always wins the fight
Forget depression, don't need the pills, this relaxing break will cure my ills
A luxury break gives us back our zest, to continue the battle to look our best
A change from giving the duster a whirl, turns "Mrs. Mop" into Wonder Girl
Such a wonderful stay in a stress-free zone, with the added advantage of a body tone
Leisure and exercise expertly blended would reduce your figure to what nature intended
Are you a harassed house husband, under pressure, who needs indulgence, rest and leisure?

Thanks to health food and spa breaks there's no mistaking,
I've got a Chippendale in the making
To reduce and firm his derriere, whilst sampling the health spa's low cal fare
Our last stubborn ounces will quickly diminish, what health food started, the spa will finish
So if you need advice and fitness checks because you look or feel like Tyrannosaurus Wrecks!
Or you're sporty, over forty and starting to fret needing every advantage you can possibly get!
I suggest a spa visit to take the 'L' out of flab, leaving you looking and feeling absolutely fab!

POEM #86
Soap Sensation

This beautiful soap makes dreams come true, leaving skin so moist, like morning dew
Its fragrance transports me on foaming clouds, to a beautiful state where luxury abounds
With its scent so heavenly, its texture divine, who'd want more in this bathroom of mine!
I can lie back dreaming of colour scheming, sunken baths and gold taps gleaming
After wallowing dozily dreaming of wealth, I then wake up wiser, glowing with health
Gently perfumed and sheer sophistication, capture luxury in this precious creation
Its value impresses me, its lather caresses me, and its fragrance de-stresses me
Surrounded by pleasure I lapse into trance – my bathroom enhancing my dreamy romance
With its luxurious scent and lather like cream, it's surely soap fit for a dream
Waking up to be pampered and petted, wallowing in its luxury couldn't be bettered
Delicate perfume so appealing, gives me that loving feeling
It goes with bidet and spas and sweet scented jars
It wins my bathroom diploma for creamy lather, exquisite aroma
For luxurious style, it leads by a mile
I feel on a par with a Hollywood star when using this heavenly soap bar
It puts a clearer complexion on my reflection, using soap and warm water for pure perfection

I am wide awake to its attributes, and wouldn't dream of using substitutes
It gives my bathroom luxurious suite dreams
Used after rising and before retiring, I find its influence most inspiring
Jacuzzi or tin bath tub, this soap is the luxury rub.
It creates a bathroom transformation, creamiest soap in the nation!
The lovely lather keeps me soft and clean, so I spend like a pauper, but bathe like a queen
It's beautifully scented and presented, to make the best soap ever invented!
Instantly at anytime of day, all worries and cares are gently soothed away.

POEM #87

The Hum Drum of Life

I've come to the conclusion and it's no illusion
That the average person is caught up in the humdrum of life

Hum Drum
Hum Drum
Hum, hum, hum, hum, drum
Hum Drum Hum Drum Hum Drum
Is caught up in the humdrum of life

By the time they get home, they have no time to roam
No wonder they moan
As they're stuck in the humdrum of life
Every new morn, I see people forlorn
Groundhog Day is reborn
As they're stuck in the humdrum of life

Hum Drum
Hum Drum
Hum, hum, hum, hum, drum
Hum Drum Hum Drum Hum Drum
Is caught up in the humdrum of life

So when you read this poetic vibe, may I suggest you join a different tribe?
Choose to think with an open heart, open your mind to a brand new start
Don't let tears cloud your vision, clarify your goals with precision
Step back from the humdrum of life!

Discard old patterns, beliefs and old trends,
Make way for curiosity, new thoughts and new friends
Live each day with smiles, love and laughter and you'll find
inner peace that lasts ever after.

POEM #88
Job Interview

I am applying for the Finance Director role that includes financial management and strategic control
Attached to this email is my current c.v. I have HR experience, marketing and IT
When megabytes meet micro brain, my business review can make it plain
When lost in jargon and each step's a bungle, I can guide the Exec Team through the accounting jungle
From laptop to iPad, from bit to byte, let my commercial skills provide the light
My results focused approach using collaborative inspiration, comfortably deals with business complexity and innovation
I can roll up my sleeves to get at grassroots or provide high-level thinking to solve problem shoots
Any work I produce will have detailed analysis commensurate with standards of 'best in class practice'
I have suitable templates for policies and procedures, personal plans, budgets and operational features
Rest assured I will manage the daily work flows and explain to those necessary to 'be in the know'
I have strategic development and planning expertise, can analyse numbers and put people at ease
As championing representative of your business's brand, I will provide commercial acumen and a 'safe pair of hands'
If you think that my 'mindset' fits with your business culture then contact me now and let's talk to each other.

POEM #89

Love All The Way!

Thank you for being here
When I am feeling my consciousness lower, my whole body and mind work much slower
I feel tense and unrelaxed. In fact, I often get a shooting pain travel right up my back
When the outlook ahead seems so bleak, it's your love and affection that I always seek
You understand my quirky ways, my stronger, happy, smiley days,
Bring me joy, leaving tears thousands of miles away
They'll be shed by someone else today
You feel me love – I don't know where it comes from – does it come from above?
You've always plenty to give and share
Make time for thanks and a little prayer
Here on earth humans act like there are limits
But with you my potential has heightened spirits
Sending me your inspiration, there is no fear or intrepidation
Love unlimited does the trick
Love unlimited heals the sick
Love, love, love, love, love, love all the way!

POEM #90
Mr. Gut Feeling

How many times do you go with the flow
And trust your body to be in the know?
Let go logic and let go science
Trust in your inner voice of defiance
That rises up against outer consciousness
And has you challenging the bullshit and senselessness
Which other people would have you believe
Makes sense of your life when it's not how you please
Know that with every decision you make
There are consequences and actions to take
The choice that you make will reflect on yourself
Your sense of purpose, self esteem and self worth
Hold your head high, cast out fear and doubt
View your reflection and feel good in and out
Pat yourself on the back, breathe in deep and stand tall
When Mr. Gut Feel's your driver there are no brick walls
To run into each time an issue arises
Only knowhow and genius, disguised as surprises
When others would have you believe their advice
Step back to observe, digest and think twice
Before committing to a wrong decision
Trust Mr. Gut Feeling and your intuition
If your solar plexus stirs and you feel instantly sick
About turn on their argument, withdraw and think quick
Push back on assumptions form your own conclusion
And know that in this moment you're reality's an illusion
Pay attention and sense what you feel in your bones
Your body's response is like a gramophone

The needle points you in the right direction
And supports each new step forward with protection
Divine love caresses and guides from within
Ensuring that unconditional love always wins
So next time you feel fear at making a decision
Know that you are guided by an inner rhythm
Just ask for help from Mr. Gut Feeling
Let him provide the response for your well-being.

POEM #91
Mark to Market

Mark to market, mark to market, mark to market
Yet no-one would admit to how it started
The trend in sales showed increased growth
Cash funds abundant pledged on oath
Yet cost of sales was understated
From work-in-progress over-rated
With each new project cash increased
Displaying profits sure to please
The money received was a five year spend
Passing through only one financial year end!
With dividends paid out and shareholders satisfied
No-one dared ask how procedures were ratified
Auditors bypassed key challenging questions
Of company performance beyond expectations
The surge in sales was much admired
By those in-house who were not fired
Yet competitors' businesses showed a decline
For those in the know, this was out of line
That a business in this industry sector could prosper
With such a return on investment offer
A random few saw decline round the bend
But for most their greed could not comprehend
That this sales treatment would only work
If the pace of business took a massive spurt
Deferred income treatment had been ignored and rejected
Younger employees keen to change this protested
Yet management's arrogance saw them ignore

Calls for balance sheet charges from across the shop floor
Instead their greed consumed their mental thought
And the company's Board filed for bankruptcy – distraught.

POEM #92
Heart of Love

He smiled in my direction as he passed by me today
And captured by intriguing charm, my heart skipped a beat.
It only took a moment to look into his eyes.
Oh love, that those bright eyes were shining, just for me.
Yet, in the passing of a second, his expression faded
And I feared silent sorrow that our love might never be...
For our lives had touched but briefly in this challenging world
Then faces blurred and cheeks flushed
A warm feeling crept into my heart
Like the glow of the sun from under a cloud
Pushing me to action,
If only to see him once more
Among the many pairs of dancing feet and seemingly endless visages
To tell him...
Were these merely illusionary dreams of love?
My heart pounded...
And before me in the loveliness of Oxford Street stood he
Arms beckoning me into his life
ME? Into his life? Could it be?
Attracting the attention of a dear friend, perhaps,
Standing behind me, or an emotional aunt – what ME?
It was me he wanted, it was me he beckoned
In reality my dreams portrayed
And so, from impulse romance blossomed
As the bud of love matures into a beauteous flower
Our lives lost to this world in the bliss of our linking hearts
Oh love, that we will never part.

POEM #93
Holiday Destinations

ALASKA – cold climate with glaciers, polar bears from a distance, nature at its best, path of least resistance;
ANTIGUA – red-hot sun, Antiguan beach and leisure, feet in the surf, a thirst-quenching treasure;
AUSTRALIA – Oz-pitality beckons, trip's a beaut, so I've labelled my baggage and crave kanga-route
BALI – videos and brochures exalt this location, blue sky retreats make for quiet contemplation
CANADA – see snow-capped mountains, crystal streams, watching wildlife – land of my dreams
CUBA – Friday night, soca music thumping, fish grilling, drinks chilling, everyone's up jumping
EGYPT – to have an incredibly bazaar time in Cairo without my mummy;
GRANADA – where the spectacular scenery, spiced with history has sugar white sand and the tingle of mystery;
GRAND CAYMAN – frequent moonlit strolls, hot sun enjoyed by day, calypso thrill, exotic play;
HAITI – while lazing under the palms with soft drink quenchers, I would imagine all those pirate adventures
JAMAICA – get reggae for beautiful beaches, tropical sunshine, and savour a glass of old oak rum that is simply divine
LAS VEGAS – as this place is open 24/7, it's a lucky gambler's seventh heaven;
LUXURY CRUISE LINER – 'steaming' into view, my laundry and ironing done by the crew, no 'pressing' engagements or filofax, just taking it easy with a view to relax;

MAURITIUS – exotic trip to paradise isle, following an ecstatic trip down the aisle;
RUSSIA – although 'red' tape decreases tourism, one thing's for certain – on a Russian cruise I'd steam through the iron curtain!
SINGAPORE – Raffles, Sentosa, Singapore Sling, together the perfect place to sing;
SNOWDONIA – 'mid beautiful mountains you can ramble all day, with food and shelter just one valley away;
SOLOMON ISLANDS – palm fringed isles, clear blue seas – my own Man Friday please!
SPACE TRIP – from space the whole world you can survey, sing David Bowie and do it the Commander Chris Hatfield way;
SPAIN – offering costas, siestas and tasty cuisine, a favourite choice for the family scene;
SWITZERLAND – with time to spare breathing in mountain air, I can indulge in chocolate without a care;
ST LUCIA – I'd love to stay by Marigot Bay and talk to the animals Dr Dolittle's way;
THE BAHAMAS – in the sexy, sultry hot Bahamas, there's no need for nighties or pyjamas;
THE GALAPAGOS ISLANDS – a protected environment makes the species on view only accessible to the privileged few;
THE LAND OF NOD – it's so much easier to fall asleep counting beaches instead of woolly sheep!
THE VIRGIN ISLES – big palms moving over me, ahh! first love, kisses, sand and sea;

TURTLE BEACH – these graceful, wise turtles know how to enjoy life at a steady pace enriched with beauty in a sacred place;
USA – State to state, the stars shine bright, on the star spangled banner with liberty in sight.

POEM #94
Today

Wild horses stand
Surveying the land
In silence,
And without a time horizon
We would do well to follow
And forget tomorrow
Take a breath and recognise what lies in the presence of NOW
All we have is the gift of NOW
Feel it, see it, sense it, be it NOW!
Yesterday is so passé
Tomorrow is another day
But stop to think of what you're doing now.
Present absence is a precursor to disease
A disconnect from one's emotions and one's right to feel at ease
Wake up, feel alive
Live for today
Without delay!
Live for today
Don't be persuaded to be led astray
Live for today
Live for today
Do it your way
And celebrate that you're alive TODAY!

POEM #95

A Box of High Life

Where did I find this new found mystery treasure
As I was tidying up one weekend at my leisure?
An old cigar box made from silky-smooth plywood
Adorned with a delicate fleur-de-lis brass hook

The box and its contents had been fast asleep in the dark
For at least fifty years untouched by a light spark
Nestled gently within a box within a box within a yellow ochre coloured suitcase
My late grandfather's memories and medals had assuredly been entangled in a dry, safe place

Torrential rain was falling outside and visibility was close to zero
Perhaps conditions similar to those experienced during both world wars by my 'Papa hero'
As he had trudged and endured unimaginable challenging complications
Known only to him on his soul journey of adventure with trepidation

As rain and hail poured down on the attic roof with an incessant rhythmic drip
It felt like I was opening a Pandora's Box about one gentleman's British Army trip
I never planned to stay long up there. Somehow time stood still and I had the situation covered.
It was time to look inside this box at the treasure trove of medals newly discovered

In celebration of one hundred years of toil, heroism and freedom
I was touching medals received in honour of fighting for one's kingdom
The history of these delicate, colourful ribbons attached to silver discs
For victories earned and battle scars amidst comrades in arms so dearly missed

'"Fall In" Answer now in your country's hour of need' was the plea for wartime volunteers
In 1914, this small, professional soldiery accepted both underage and overage men regardless of their years
If you exist, then please enlist and get on to the team
The British Army needs you to raise this nation's self-esteem

At the innocent age of fourteen having lied about his age, my Papa had voluntarily enlisted out of duty and care
In France and Belgium he had been trained on the prevailing conditions of trench warfare
Among the growing mass citizen army detailed attack practice was carried out in both small and large formations
Tactics and technologies of the war were very quickly developed which were seen as necessary innovations

My Papa had always smoked his pipe using Condor Ready Rubbed
With scars of old war memories forever mindful like a bathtub after being constantly scrubbed

I often watched him take out his tobacco from the cellophane pouch and pack it into his well-worn pipe before striking it alight
And puff, puff, puffing it contentedly with an expression of putting the world to right

Each time I visited my Papa at his home he hugged me in a warm embrace
And walked me in silence up the thirteen stairs to his attic office with a stern face
We sat down at his wooden desk as he faithfully and quietly reached for a tin
To show me his carefully preserved World War 1 digestive ration biscuit therein

I would fondly gaze into my Papa's eyes and often held the 'concrete' biscuit in my hand
Forever grateful that he'd survived two World Wars that I would never truly understand
Now it is time for us to know that in the remembrance comes the light
And the awareness of the test of energy between darkness and light without the need to fight

In this important time of planetary shift we are headed for peace on earth
For those now being born they know this is 'a given' from birth
Deep in your sacred heart you too know that the light quotient is winning

Finally, we are destined on planet earth for a peace-filled new beginning

While I am unable to give a personal account of the course of my Papa's events
I do know that the trauma and pain of war no longer make for common sense
Sharing our wisdom and living in peace, let's bring countries together in celebration
With the expectation that warring will cease, we could form an Alliance of Nations?

Section 3
Esoteric Truths

It is so important for you to know that you are never alone
When you wave friends goodbye and put down your phone
There's a whole new world waiting for you filled with love and respect
Only with your free choice are they allowed to connect
This invisible reality is your connection to truth
It is open to everyone and is your birthright to youth
I am so happy to share this esoteric information
That has been passed down and known by the indigenous generations
In year five of a new esoteric epoch it is time
For souls to awaken to their truth sublime
Let serendipitous adventures hold you in admiration
May the synchronicity of your life flow in endless celebration
For when you listen to the whispers deep inside your heart
You will be guided to drop your ego and make a brand new start!
Make a sacred promise to yourself to be your best
Embrace life's challenges and pass the energy test
This time is all about the discovery of self
Will you rise to the challenge and enjoy active health and wealth?

POEM #96

Feel the Freedom

Background

I have often admired the design of Glasgow born architect Charles Rennie McIntosh. After a recent visit to The House of an Art Lover, I was inspired by the beautiful fragrant flowers and garden displays in the House's grounds in Bellahouston Park. It really made me feel appreciative of the natural smells, sights and signature notes of flowers and trees that can be enjoyed for free.

POEM #96
Feel the Freedom

Feel the freedom
Take a breath
Connect with inner happiness

Don't judge others
Be yourself
Believe your path to inner health

Save some pennies
Treat yourself
Trust your right to access wealth

Standing still
Destroys your life
Breathe deeply and let go of strife

Think of others
Throw a smile
Let your actions speak your style!

POEM #97

Perfect Peace

Background

At the close of each of my two compassionate care books I wrote lyrics as a contribution to my first album project. In the 'Feel The Love' tips book Volume 1 When Visiting Someone in Hospital to offer readers an improved healing experience for their loved-one, my poem (lyrics) was titled 'Perfect Peace'.

When you have a friend, a close family member, relative or colleague in hospital, the first thing you notice as a visitor is how it 'changes' your world and your daily routine. This, alone, may become very stressful as each of us seeks to juggle life's challenges.

Perfect Peace was written to focus our minds on the joy and gratitude that we can take from the beauty and simplicity of living and breathing every minute of every day in love, free from any individual obsession with material things and/ or perceived stress and drama that we choose to cloud our minds.

POEM #97

Perfect Peace
(lyrics)

When music sings its song of love and draws you to attention
Listen to the impact that it has on your affection
For the joy of life, that each day brings
Without the need for material things,
Should never be neglected,
But be cherished, honoured and protected.
So next time when you breathe in air
Breathe in hope and not despair,
Know that love will get you there
Live your life in peace.

POEM #98

I Am Always in The Right Place

Background

I love the spontaneity with which poetry and lyrics are channelled to me. One morning on a visit to Edinburgh, I was waiting patiently at the train station when the first two lines of this song popped into my head. At first I thought I would remember these words, but then within seconds I could feel there were even more to follow. My train was only minutes away from pulling into the station. What would be best to do to avoid forgetting them? I could see the train approaching and started to search for my mobile phone inside my handbag.

On board the train I found a quiet group of seats and facing out to the window I recorded the words into my phone. A tune was coming through at the same time. It was magical! Within about five to ten minutes my work was done! Enjoy!

POEM #98

I Am Always in The Right Place (lyrics)

I am always in the right place at the right time
I am always walking where I need to be
Love permeates all life that is around me
Mother Nature and all things I cannot see

For love's a universal quantum feeling
That feeling deep inside can't be denied
I am always in the right place at the right time
With a guarantee of help that I will find

I am always in the right place at the right time
I am always walking where I need to be
There's no need to be alone when you're connected
An open heart, love and compassion are the key

For love's a universal quantum feeling
That feeling deep inside can't be denied
I am always in the right place at the right time
With a guarantee of help that I will find

I am always in the right place at the right time
I am always walking where I need to be
That palatable force is strong and present
A guiding light within and around me

For love's a universal quantum feeling
That feeling deep inside can't be denied
I am always in the right place at the right time
With a guarantee of LOVE that I will find
A guarantee of LOVE
A guarantee of LOVE
A guarantee of LOVE that I will find

POEM #99

Expect The Unexpected!

Background

The summer of 2018 in Scotland was exceptional. Light is information and so I choose to be outside in the sunshine as often as I can. The recent warm weather encouraged many people to spend more time outdoors and walking amongst nature than they may otherwise have done with wetter conditions.

One of the ways that we can raise our vibration and spiritually evolve is to reconnect with Pachamama, Gaia, Mother Earth.

The indigenous peoples have always respected the earth and known that their ancestors came from the stars. Disappointingly, many cultures and peoples have grown up without an appreciation for our planet until now. Thankfully, due to more people speaking their truth during the thirty-six year cycle of the Precession of the Equinoxes and the positive impact of social media, there is now a heightened awareness of the significance of our entangled relationship with our planet.

Since 21 December 2012 when humanity on planet earth was propelled into Graduate Status, we can all look forward to 'expecting the unexpected' as the invisible galactic and universal energies work with those humans on planet earth who have love, integrity and compassion at heart in all they do.

POEM #99

Expect The Unexpected!

What affects one part of your body, affects the whole
Know your right to truth and love, embrace your soul
Thank you Mr. Sun for feeding me with light
I know deep in my heart that the future is bright

Expect the unexpected
Connect to the divine
Know you are protected
And this is your time!

Smart individuals put their 'dumb' phones away
Venture out into nature where they laugh, dance, sing and play
Talk to the animals, appreciate the trees
Take time to look at butterflies, buttercups and bees

Expect the unexpected
Connect to the divine
Know your right to be here
Break the barrier of time!

Do you know your poplars from an ash and a beech?
Have you held a tadpole, stroked a spider, felt a leech?
Reconnect with these precious, luscious, verdant lands,
Visit neighbouring beaches dressed in fine, golden sands

Expect the unexpected
Know this is your time
You deserve to be here
And to live a life sublime!

How often do you take the chance to look up at the stars?
Use a telescope to view planetary systems such as Mars
Absorb the beauty of the skies, dream of worlds you cannot see
Welcome to the world of me!

Expect the unexpected
Live in joy and liberty
You have a right to truth and love
This is your destiny!

POEM #100

In Divine Time

Background

The words to this poem were channelled during the night. Fortunately I had a pen and notebook to hand to write them down. I particularly like the title because as human beings we are often so impatient to do things or to wait for results or outcomes to what we want in life.

When each of us becomes more aware of our connection to the universe, we better understand that what we think is the right time for something to happen is often at variance with when the time is right according to the universe and synchronicity. Patience is a virtue. It is for us to relax and allow the potentials of what we dream and desire to come to fruition. With more than seven billion people on planet earth it can take a little longer for everything to be put in place. Yet, when we give pure intention for something then the universe has to comply. Be careful what you wish for! Ha! Ha!

POEM #100
In Divine Time

Remember your power to dream and create
Retain inspiration and hope as you wait
It's too easy to quit and deny your success
Just because you're impatient to achieve your best

In divine time
You'll get a sign
In divine time
Life is sublime

When you choose to laugh you opt not to cry
The positive energies allow you to fly
All fears are dropped and you love from the heart
It's your free choice to make a fresh start

In divine time
You'll get a sign
In divine time
Life is sublime

Your heart activator connects with your soul
The inner and the outer matter make you whole
Humanity's evolving to create a world of truth
Where compassion is in fashion and its cool for you to youth

New science proves the answers are a change in DNA
With an extra pair of chromosomes a miracle's at play
We can heal with higher consciousness and never need a pill
That's the strength of human spirit coupled with an iron will

In divine time
You'll get a sign
In divine time
Life is sublime
Life is sublime
Life is sublime!

POEM #101
Beyond the Illusion

Background

The dark, old energy dominated planet earth until 21 December 2012, when we reached a tipping point. More people than ever before have now decided in the depths of their heart that they want to live in peace. There are wonderful invisible energies that are loving and helping humanity to attain peace on earth. It all starts with you and how you feel and your every thought, word and action. Old energy still exists on the planet but those people who decide with freewill to be compassionate, kind and loving human beings will outshine them and outsmart them.

In Old Energy, one has a tendency to be arrogant, feel stuck in one's life and feel limited in what can be achieved.

In New Energy, one has a tendency to be ever learning, activating new ideas with one's creativity and imagination and feeling unlimited in the scope of what is possible to achieve.

Old Energy is based in the energy of the Age of Pisces and is synonymous with mental instability, delusion, confusion, illusion, divinity and hidden truth.

In addition, sadly we are witnessing mass disruption from across the world at all levels from individuals who are at dis-ease with whom they are and who are struggling to find their own authenticity in their life. Without understanding of their 'being' and the reconnection to the 'love power' inside of them, many become so confused that they resort to negative,

destructive acts that leave a trail of sadness, loss and broken hearts, forever scarred. You see the power of this divine spark that is within each human being has as much power to destroy as it has to passionately love. Part of the puzzle of life is for us to choose, with freewill, either a life based in love or a life that is fear based and negative. It is all up to YOU!

POEM #101
Beyond The Illusion

The blackbird sings his song at dawn
As I wake up with stifled yawn
Feel the listening of the Earth's heartbeat
Can you hear the music of the blackbird's tweet
Greet your awakening to a brand new dawn?
Stretching your legs and feet with a yawn
Sense the stirring of the Earth's heartbeat
As you sit up now and take your seat
Among the blackbirds, swallows chaffinches and thrush
All eager to start this new day in a rush...
Of enthusiasm, elated at a brand new day
Ready to start new beginnings in a whole different way
The code is given in each musical note
And interpreted from birds to animals to folk
Make no mistake these are good vibrations
Raising frequencies across the nations
Speaking of love, emotions and personal power
Hungrily recaptured in each waking hour
The trilling sounds send out a call
Awaken and embody your new found freedom
As each creature has done in the animal kingdom
Understand and respect your sense of self-worth
For this personal power has belonged to you since birth
Allow your heart to set you free
Be all of you in me that you see (that you can be)
For the 'isness' of all that is I AM
Beckons you be true to YOU and wake up to the sham!

POEM # 102
Feel a Touch of Love

Background

In keeping with my plan to finish each compassionate care book written with song lyrics, I had these wonderful words channelled to me which complete my 'Feel The Love' book Volume 2 When Caring For Someone at Home.

After the death of my beloved mother I found it very difficult to find meaning to my life. We had both been each other's best friend since my late father's death some years earlier and to suddenly be without her physically in my life was a major blow.

I have, however, always believed that the soul was eternal and that when we love someone it transcends linear time. After my father's passing I often felt his presence and even now he still visits me in my dreams.

Today I have acquired more knowledge and I am wiser about the birth and death cycles of every human being than I was when I wrote my first two books. The one specific attribute that loved-ones who have passed on want their relatives and friends to know is that they are not dead, their souls are alive and they are desperate to speak with you. This communication comes in many forms. They hear you when you speak to their photographs in your home, at their gravestone, when you are in bed and in your prayers. Can't you FEEL their presence around you? Talk to them whenever you want! They exist beyond the three dimensional, linear reality in which we conduct most of our life until we

WAKE UP. They surround you and send you healing when you need it.

As you read this poem please keep an open heart about your loved-ones who want to connect with you and 'Feel a Touch of Love'.

POEM # 102

Feel a Touch of Love (Lyrics)

Though I no longer hear you talk I feel your touch when oft I walk
I know that you still come to share my new life now and say a prayer
That I will learn to love again, work through the stress, work through the pain
To let go anger, let go fear, and live in hope and love each year

Will you smile with me forever?
Will you laugh with me forever?
Will you cry with me forever?
Know our souls will always be together
Forever, forever, forever, "feel the love!"

When you ascended I lost my direction all feelings of love, life and genuine affection
The decision to live had to come from me, my awakening came when you set me free
I start each day with gratitude, greet those I meet with love and attitude
The time is now, so find a way, make your day count and don't delay!

Will you smile with me forever?
Will you laugh with me forever?
Will you cry with me forever?
Know our souls will always be together
Forever, forever, forever, "feel the love!"

Just like a diamond with each flawless facet, love everlasting is a priceless asset
To give a hug or smile in care, spotlights the love that people can share
Look within and cherish and treasure, the kisses and hugs that you give without measure
Lighten your heart and love yourself; the healing has started to wisdom and wealth

Know you smile with me forever
Know you laugh with me forever
Know you cry with me forever
Know our souls are always linked together
Forever, forever, forever, "feel the love!"

POEM # 103
Duality

Background

What is the meaning of life? We are in a test of energy between dark and light. Essentially when we raise our consciousness we also raise the amount of light that is in our bodies. How do we do this? We do this by activating our heart. We connect more to our emotions and feelings that have often been suppressed by our previous experiences in life.

I want you to know that you can free yourself by feeling the love that is within you and feel the love inside that you have for you. Only when you can truly love yourself first, can you then love others. It is your birthright! Look within to break out of the mode of duality into colour, light, love and new possibilities for you!

POEM # 103
Duality

Each moment in your life brings a new possibility
Based on your connection to inner peace and tranquility
This means that you can positively influence your life
When you drop all emotions and feelings of strife
Embrace love, compassion, kindness, laughter and joy
Take a leaf out of wise words spoken by Tolstoy
"The kingdom of God is within us" has meaning
There's no mystery involved, it all depends on your feelings

It's long been known that the choices you make
Are based on the quality of DNA that you generate
The test on planet earth is a test for humanity
To choose between dark and light called duality
With belief we can will ourselves any outcome to surpass
We are magnificent vibrating beings of energy mass
Who also have an invisible field around us called innate
Which together with our heart and mind, cause us at different frequencies to vibrate
We are awakening to who we are that blends scientific proof with spirituality
Defined in the Changeover Years with creating peace and healing in a new reality.

POEM #104
Heartbeat of Life

Background

How much attention do you pay to birds flying around your home? Do you hear the dawn chorus? Perhaps you own a pet? How often do you truly listen to different sounds? Have you ever listened to your own heart beat in the stillness of the night?

I woke up during the night and started listening to my heart beating. It was so beautiful. Later that morning after I had fully awakened I looked out my bedroom window and watched a hawk flying high above in the sky. Within seconds I could feel more words forming in my head and 'Heartbeat of Life' was birthed.

One of the ways to better understand who we are is to reconnect with nature as often as possible. Our feelings for nature come from a loving heart. The strengthening of this bond and appreciation helps us to improve our awareness and intuition.

POEM #104
Heartbeat of Life

Listen to your heartbeat like a rhythmic beating drum
Signalling the happiness and joy of life to come
Take pleasure from each sunset and the rising sun
And know deep in your heart that life is great
Know deep in your heart that life is great

Listen to your heartbeat
It's the sound of being alive
Listen to your heartbeat
It's the key for you to thrive!
Key for you to thrive
Key for you to thrive
Feel the love inside
Sound of being alive
Sound of being alive!

Observe the freedom of the hawks as they fly above
Relax your soul, intuit your own journey of endless love
Feel the joy within your heart, contentment of a dove
And know deep in your heart that life is great
Know deep in your heart that life is great

Listen to your heartbeat
It's the sound of being alive
Listen to your heartbeat
It's the key for to thrive!
Key for you to thrive

Key for you to thrive
Feel the love inside
Sound of being alive
Sound of being alive!

Forever is a circle just like rainbows in the sky
Through the spectrum of your light within, your soul can never die
Speak your truth, be proud of you and hold your head up high
And know deep in your heart that life is great
Know deep in your heart that life is great

Your heart is the connector to the source of everything
When you drop all fear and sadness you allow your heart to sing
Close you eyes for a moment, stand still and take a deep breath in
And know deep in your heart that life is great
Know deep in your heart that life is great

Your heart is the connector to the source of life itself
Your heart is the connector to your active health and wealth
You are the master builder of the best life for yourself
You know deep in your heart that life is great
Know deep in your heart that life is great

Listen to your heartbeat
It's the sound of being alive
Listen to your heartbeat
It's the key for you to thrive!
Key for you to thrive
Key for you to thrive
Feel the love inside
Sound of being alive
Sound of being alive!

POEM #105
A Superhuman Redefined

Background

There are various rights that every human being has which have been overlooked in society.

Whether you believe it or not, every human being is on earth on their own spiritual journey.

We have the right to live in joy and abundance every day.

When a human being reconnects inside with their Higher Self, Higher Guidance, God, Creator Source or that divine spark within by another name, they remember more of who they are and have access to talents, gifts and skills that are in their Akash (more about this is explained in my book, 'Know Who You Are!'). This is what differentiates the power between what we presently consider is normal for a human being and the new superhuman.

POEM #105
A Superhuman Redefined

I have the right to be here
I have the right to truth
I have the right to who I am
I have the right to youth

I have the right to knowledge
And to know what's going on
I have the right to education.

I have the right to feel love
I have the right to act
I have the right to speak my truth
The right to know the facts

I have the right to my beliefs
In my own spiritual way
I have the right to live in joy each day.

I have the right to inner peace
A heart that's void of fear
I have the right to liberate
And manifest dreams here

I become superhuman with each intake of air
And exhale all negativity
When I look in the mirror and see who I am
I raise my self-esteem with dignity

I feel the bliss of God inside
I do not need to see
I am grateful I have found my truth
I relax and simply be.

I claim my rights of mastery
I am the master of my mind
I am a superhuman redefined.

POEM #106

Be True!

Background

One of the unexplained mysteries to life is to love with all your heart and to do what makes you happy. When you follow your passion and are authentic to this truth, your life forever changes for the better.

POEM #106

Be True!

Stand your ground
Know your mind
And you will find
Things all come together
You can't give in
If you're to win
Giving up is a sin
The greater your strength the better
If you play the ace card
It won't be that hard
Start in your own backyard
And build from there
The ace's card is your face
Coupled with grace
Always know there's a place
For you to prosper
Stand your ground
There's no need to be scared
The key is in being prepared
Now that you have found your breakthrough
Doors will open up for you
Your success will be a coup
Remember, it's only possible when you can 'Be True!'

POEM #107

The 'Love Power' of YOU!

Background

This poem accompanies my book "Love IS The Way!" which was inspired from viewing the Royal Wedding of 'Meghan and Harry' on 19 May 2018. Know that inspiration can come from anywhere and often from the most unlikely sources!

The book focuses on the core truth of love and is non-religious. I have expanded on my own personal vision of how, together, we can choose to live in greater harmony, balance and love in this remarkable world.

It is encouragement for you to resist listening to old energy patterning and trusting old systems that are no longer working for humanity in the New Era. Many individuals still live their daily lives in fear and believe that there is a possibility of World War Three. Please be assured that the tipping point for this potentiality occurring was 21 December 2012 when humanity passed the marker. We are headed for peace! Have hope and trust your intuition. Stop listening to the old energy broadcasts put out. Yes, there may be a few small wars that take place as individuals and citizens within countries start to jostle for new ways of doing things which go against the 'old guard' who are entrenched in their traditional systems and ways of doing things. Have you noticed recently how any fighting that takes place is generally within countries as people decide what they want from the government of their own countries, rather than fighting among countries as used to be the way?

The best way to raise the consciousness of this planet is to focus on your own spiritual evolution. The simple message of this poem is for you to find the love within your heart and feel the 'Love Power' of YOU!

POEM #107

The 'Love Power' of YOU!

We are expanding our minds beyond linear time
As we change our ways from the past to the sublime
Never in history has there been such an adventure
But how much of the changeover can you absorb without censure?
For the nano years have been and gone
No more Armageddon we choose to live on
The way forward is to trust your intuition
And your inner knowing without inhibition
Learn to find your natural way
Of living life in your truth each day
Stand grounded in your chosen path
Be not persuaded by another's wrath
Let old conditioning patterns go
And practise being grounded and "in the know!"
Release emotional tensions of old
And allow your "journey of feeling" to unfold
Demand freedom to explore what you want to do
Surrender and truly feel The 'Love Power' of YOU!
Acknowledge what is keeping you stuck and LET GO
Reassess and change your perspective of how your life will best flow
Strengthen your connection to nature
Open your eyes and WAKE UP to the adventure
Decide on your future and follow your dream
Know that at ALL times you are guided by spirits unseen
Who have your best interests and heart wholly supported
No matter what outside nonsense is reported

Start walking your truth, feel the vibrancy within
Strengthen your voice and never give in
Step into your awesomeness, stand tall in your power
Know that you are loved more and more by the hour.

POEM #108
Cosmic Connections

Background

The joy of channelling for me up until now is that I never know when the words are going to flow. This beautiful poem came through within an hour of writing out another poem and so I was already seated at my laptop for the words to be channelled and typed up.

When we are fully connected to the multi-dimensional parts of ourselves then we are often given messages and solutions to our problems in our dreams, or encouraged to use our senses more, such as feeling the truth of a predicament with our gut feeling to determine how comfortable we are with a particular situation. This poem has been channelled as though the information has come through as a dream.

Many people struggle to remember the dreams that they have. May I suggest that when you can relate to this comment, take a pen and notepaper to keep at your bedside. Do not worry when you have a dream and still cannot remember it sufficiently to write it down. Be patient! In divine time you will be become accustomed to remembering what you need to remember and spirit will work with you to give you more information. As you place your focus on remembering and writing down your dreams, more information will be given to you. Writing down your dreams is just one signal to the universe that you are paying attention to the invisible energies that are here to love, support and help you in your life.

POEM #108
Cosmic Connections

I dreamt that planet Earth, Mother Gaia, two hundred thousand years ago was truly a beautiful place
She was easily reached from other Galaxies and accepting of all 'Extra Terrestrials' and every living species and race
Prime Creator boldly brought many energies and essences of life into this Universe as a mass project of human evolution
Yet, certain created warriors were fighting to control this Living Library of free will and reduce it to darkness using a variegated form of DNA pollution
For eons, a single radio frequency had everyone's DNA restricted,
Shutting off ten strands of an optimum twelve DNA, with only two depicted
Now it is time to revitalise the higher self and take courage,
For with twelve helixes of DNA in place each "being" will flourish
Light is information and darkness is lack of light
The sunlight brings the freedom to evolve with each passing night
The humanoid aliens tell me this revolution of consciousness must be done together
What happens on Earth now will change all Universes forever
I am told to sit up, take notice and have a sense of self worth
Love is everything. Love is the elixir of life
Perception is everything here on Mother Earth
The emotion of love is the emotion in which we were created

Until now we have been confused, distracted from exploring emotion, placated

'Seek unity in all you do, knowing that to do one's best keeps you true.'

I awaken into an infinite field of unimaginable, unlimited possibilities! The physics of LOVE! A magnificent system of LOVE. All LOVE... benevolent help for mankind

It is the LOVE and the EVOLution of humanity called the Esoteric Era! A quest for every human being to look within and a child of the galaxy to find.

POEM #109
Celebrate YOU!

Background

One of the main factors that holds us back from success, abundance, joy, love and happiness in our life is our lack of self-esteem and self-respect for ourselves. It is as if some individuals want to deliberately sabotage their own success because they have been told as a child that they are not worthy, they are undeserving of such happiness and that success is for other people to attain and achieve with joy. Sadly, all of these excuses and reasons are untrue. Spirit sees each of us as perfect as we live and progress on our own spiritual journey called life. I would like you as a reader of this poem to know that you are magnificent. You are the greatest unique YOU that there is on planet earth!

POEM #109
Celebrate YOU!

On this brand new day feel your confidence soar,
Embrace self-esteem and self-worth even more
Be assertive in your expression,
Ignore negative influencers and change your direction
Be true to you in saying what you think
Remain self-balanced and allow your ego to shrink
For inside you is a spark divine
Take a deep breath and reach heights sublime
Make no assumptions and go with the flow
Harness your wisdom and know as you go
You are so worthy of each act you do
Stand tall, be yourself and be proud of YOU!

POEM #110
Full Creative Control

Background

This is one of my more serious poems which imparts much information for you to absorb, challenge and decide for yourself why some or all about what I am writing is resonating a deep truth within your heart. I want to encourage and inspire you to understand that your mind is not your master. You have Full Creative Control!

POEM #110
Full Creative Control

What if you were told you had full creative control?
That this is the best time in history for you to be YOU and watch your talents unfold
For the first time in human civilisation it's time to separate the unreal from the real
And create new realities from darkness to light based on how you really feel
For when you follow the feeling, you can build brand new beliefs
Understanding that you are the 'creating creator' of your life is a tremendous relief
No more reliance on the promise of a prophet returned
It's entirely up to you to create the glorious life for which you've yearned
Believe in yourself for every human has been granted a piece of divinity by the Creator
Use this gift wisely, humbly and in gratitude bestowed on you as it is to make you an innovator
How often have you sat next to someone who makes you feel good;
Who raised your self-worth, took time to listen to you and understood;
Who accepted you for who you are and made no judgement when you spoke;
In whose company you felt at ease, oblivious to time and the surrounding folk?
What qualities in them allowed you in them your secrets to trust?
Was it their calmness of presence, appreciation of nature or simply their aura of love?

When we can advance beyond ego, discernment and patience will guide our way
We can become more resourceful with a purity of heart that enjoys both work and play
For judgement is always cruel and robs us of our truth
Judgement is a "cancer" in humanity that can deprive us of great youth
It feeds off a deficiency, a lack of self-worth and a mask for true feeling
The arrogance of judgement finding one person lovable and another unlovable is unbalanced and sets other reeling!
There is the ability in every human being to be "flawsome"
A blend of being flawed in some ways, while in others being awesome!
The beauty of a balanced person is your desire to be around them
For they travel their journey with love, trust, forgiveness, connectedness and wisdom
They attach to their truth and then step back detached
This allows them to see the pattern, observe and then have synchronicities matched
To the many possibilities and potentials of desires to be fulfilled
Created in their mind with purity of heart and focused energy willed
They consider the needs of others and are loving and kind
Yet, in illuminating their heart's vitality they also know their own mind

They are practical and happy to make friends with the word, "No!"
Prioritising what is important and what is a distraction are keys to letting go
With an innate wisdom to know that all things are sentient
For life exists in a myriad of forms which are all transient
Take the seed of a flower as it grows, buds, blossoms and dies
And unlocks its radiance and beauty each day before your very eyes
This freedom of life can be attained by you too, it's a matter of perspective
Take responsibility for your own journey and in your own life be introspective
Who are you? Why are you here? You are unique and here to live your best life
There's no more need for pain, dis-ease, struggle, anxiety and strife
These days of hard, hard slog can now be put behind you, when you have faith in YOU!
It's about recognising your divinity and the divinity in everything and all that you do
You are an immortal creature of planet Earth and of this solar system and its greater galaxies' structure
At this time in human evolution called "The Shift" you have the power to create a new culture.
Remember that when you take the path of light and clear visibility
It is important that you protect yourself at all times from hostility

From other human beings who have chosen to remain unhealed
And in whose company your energy force field may naturally yield
In a way that melds your aura and creates an interference
Thereby eroding your own power and your beautiful magnificence.
So to safeguard your strength of power, keep your own force field strong
"Aura, up, up, up!" and surround yourself with three layers of golden protection to ensure energy vampires are begone
As you slowly restructure your own paradigm of reality
You will create new pathways of consciousness out of joy and joviality
New options and new ways of loving and living will develop
When you can the new framework for quantum dimensional thinking, embrace and envelop
Each person who creates this evolutionary leap in the body starts to produce a strong trend
That one by one begins to impact the world and sees war come to an end!
The gentle hand of peace stretched out across Mother Earth will become the "new normal"
Peace will come to reign in the silence and invisibility of the seeming paranormal
It does not come in a hailstone of bullets but in the stillness of the dawn
When you lie fast asleep only to wake up to the glory of each new morn.

The air of tranquility is broken with the birdsong vibration
Awakening nature and humanity to a fresh day of celebration
Can you feel the energy change across the earth?
As frequencies rise and Mother Gaia is given new birth
Lay lines are being reenergised and obelisks reactivated
To bring them back into balance as old energy is annihilated
The Old Earth is filled with misinformation, lies, empty rhetoric and deception
To those human beings who rise above the nonsense of 3D there is a changed perception
Where the third dimensional state of the planet fades away
As the first domino falls and the knock-on effect gains a momentum cast astray
By the careful orchestration of a New Earth form
The Moon calls for courage entrancing a soul on fire for truth that is stubborn,
Stubborn in its desire to balance the need for freedom with its duties
Yet concerned by its path and rigidity of knowing what its route is
In this new energy, it is time to let go and make no assumptions, simply know as you go
Find the missing link that connects you with the greatest of compassion
Honour your precious life in love and grace and learn to fulfil your passion
Mother Gaia is coming out of her confinement and shining with grace

Ready for you to open up yourself to new possibilities and the unknown to embrace
When you speak your truth as beautiful as you can
You improve the silence of every living person on the land
Remember the power of words and the power of intention
Are two great forces for co-creating new inventions
When you plan intuitively use a feeling of "rightness" as your best guide
Working out what makes you happy will fill you with pleasure and pride
There's plenty of need for a garage tinkerer who can do for himself
Welding steel, aluminium and galvanised parts off the shelf.
When the human spirit is ready to surrender to divine order
The body, spirit and innate meld with one another and reveal a world of splendour
We are all equal and the power lies within
What makes your heart sing and not sink is your indicator to begin
To love yourself and let go limiting beliefs
With a soul that is free and answerable to no chiefs...
But YOU! So fully embrace the present moment wherever you may be
And work the data that you have as your plan of inner mastery
The greatest challenge of all is the love challenge and that of self-actualisation
Possible when you first love yourself and become fully aligned with your piece of divination

Each of us has the free choice to be aligned to highest light
To transmute every negative thought, link, alliance or connection out of sight
Into the ether; so you can develop into a greater state of purity
In accordance with divine order and your natural being of unity
When you remove yourself from the glamour of the material world
Your positive etheric body will receive knowledge, truths and attributes will be unfurled
Disengaging from the dominant out-of-balance forces of matter for your spiritual evolution
Allows your heightened senses and intention to improve your use of creative imagination
Create, create, create with the use of Higher Self, your intuition and innate
Know that at all times you have full creative control, embrace your divinity and thrive 'Old Soul'!

POEM #111
Love Is Contagious!

Background

For the first time in our history on planet earth we have triggered a renaissance of humanity. Planet earth has now achieved Graduate Status. This means that we are on our way to becoming a more loving, compassionate civilisation and peace on earth is a given.

We are in year 5 of a New Earth with more and more people awakening to the power and magnificence of who they are every day. Until 2027 we are in a one-time only acceleration window or fast-track opportunity to remember who we are.

Part of the joy of this new era is that love is contagious! How amazing is this? I think it is so wonderful and so funny all at once, because when we have pure love for others they become 'infected' with love too! That is worth writing about.

POEM #111

Love Is Contagious!

Pure love is contagious
Whether you like it or not
It's completely outrageous
I'm taking mine back to the shop!

Love implants a potential
For you to grow in your heart
It's the basic essential
For Gaia to make a new start

Forget about watching mainstream news
Create your own joy from your love within
Drop all negativity and judgemental views
Know you are worthy and never give in!

Pure love is contagious
It doesn't care if you object
It's completely infectious
And never circumspect

Love imbues your open heart
To feelings and emotions
Inspires you to better things
With passion and devotion

Conclusion

I hope you will find these poems nourish
Your inner being that's so keen to flourish
Feel the hero in you and have fun with each one
May these words inspire you in who you can become!

Kindness with attitude
Shows love and gratitude
We are one vibration, one heart, one tribe
Thank you for helping me spread this vibe!

About the Author

Lady Wise is an influential new voice and a Wayshower in the exciting Esoteric Era in which we now find ourselves.

She is a heart-centred entrepreneur, life and business strategist, Chartered Accountant, inspirational speaker, singer/songwriter and author who is passionate about improving the healing and living experience of individuals. It is her dream for every individual to feel that they are fulfilling their potential in life and living the best version of themselves. She inspires and assists human beings on their journey of self-discovery and personal transformation to understand their own life purpose.

"

Never allow anyone to dampen your spirit

For you are divine and Mother Earth needs you on it!

~ Lady Wise

Other Books of Interest

ESOTERIC BOOKS

Love IS The Way!

Do you act on your gut feeling too? This book was inspired from viewing the Royal Wedding of 'Meghan and Harry' on 19 May 2018. Know that inspiration can come from anywhere and often from the most unlikely sources!

The book focuses on the core truth of love and is non-religious. I have expanded on my own personal vision of how, together, we can choose to live in greater harmony, balance and love in this remarkable world.

I hope to encourage you to connect with the love that is inside of you to become a happier, balanced and calmer person living in harmony and love wherever you are and doing whatever you choose to do. I appreciate that each of us must 'self-motivate' to be empowered. We must each create with total clarity of mind what it is that we want coupled with a sense of deserving, love and graciousness.

We have allowed ourselves over the generations to close off our emotions as human beings and thereby deprive ourselves of the greatest joy on planet earth that one can imagine – the joy of feeling, expressing and giving love!

Enjoy, embrace the truth and be exuberant in creating your own success, abundance and happiness through the joy of 'love power' and expect the unexpected!

A catalogue record for this book is available from the British Library.

Paperback: ISBN: 978-0-9933513-4-1

EBook: ISBN: 978-0-9933513-5-8

"KNOW WHO YOU ARE!"

Due for release 2020

For more than twenty years I have been especially curious about life, my life, and who I truly am in an esoteric, metaphysical way. This has led to several epiphanies of laughter, joy, love and self-discovery! I am passionate about imparting my knowledge when appropriate to others and allowing the free choice of every human being to further question and know who they are.

When my uncle in Australia fell seriously ill in 2016, I felt a compelling need to write to him and impart what I had learned about the puzzle of life. I intuitively believe that every single lifetime builds a library of wisdom and I wanted to share this esoteric knowledge with him, 'old soul' to 'old soul' before his physical departure from planet Earth.

I started to write to him most mornings and evenings and have modified the letters slightly for ease of delivery into 111 letters for you to read. These letters are of a personal story unfolding between two 'old souls'. I hope this book will be a source of inspiration to those individuals seeking their own truth of existence, enabling them to better understand their reason for being.

With greater insight into our spiritual existence, each one of us can stand in our truth and enhance our intuition using our sacred heart. The beauty of life itself can be yours!

"GOOD HEALTH IS THE NEW WEALTH!"

Due for release 2020

In such challenging times as we move through the heart of the Changeover Years (2013-2027), we are encouraged to go within ourselves and introspectively better understand who we are. This is the essence to recognising our own roadmap for good health and abundance and empowering ourselves to make the best choices for how we want to thrive.

When we experience a life free from dis-ease, we are able to flourish as creative beings of love. We expect to live each day in harmony with other human beings and with nature that promotes inner peace and well-being. From this state of balance we are able to live a joy-filled life of compassion, active health and wealth!

COMPASSIONATE CARE BOOKS

FEEL THE LOVE
VOLUME 1
111 Tips
WHEN VISITING SOMEONE IN HOSPITAL

Want to solve an immediate problem for your friend or loved one who is in hospital and are unsure how to help?

Are you unconsciously increasing the anxiety of your loved-one in hospital?

Would you like to reduce the stress of visiting a vulnerable relative in hospital?

111 tips are broken down into eleven chapters to help reduce stress for both in-patients and visitors, as witnessed through the eyes of a 'carer' with no medical qualifications but a passion for improving your healing experience.

A catalogue record for this book is available from the British Library.

Paperback: ISBN: 978-0-9933513-2-7

EBook: ISBN: 978-0-9933513-0-3

FEEL THE LOVE VOLUME 2 111 Tips WHEN CARING FOR SOMEONE AT HOME

Want to solve an immediate problem for your friend or loved one who is still living at home and are unsure how to help?

111 tips are broken down into eleven chapters to help reduce stress for both you and your loved one, as witnessed through the eyes of an unpaid 'carer' with no medical qualifications but a passion for improving the healing and living experience at home.

A catalogue record for this book is available from the British Library.

Paperback: ISBN: 978-0-9933513-3-4

EBook: ISBN: 978-0-9933513-1-0

Lady Wise is keen to extend the 'FEEL THE LOVE' series of books as a source of inspiration to those individuals seeking more hope, love and compassion in their daily lives.

Finance and Business Strategy

"BLENDED FINANCE" (SERIES OF 6 E-BOOKS)

This series of business & financial books targets Business Owners and Managers, Entrepreneurs and Directors who have been in business for at least two years, who are keen to accelerate business performance and continue to grow a sustainable company in the new era of compassion!

Volume 1 "Look After Your Assets!" gives you greater insight into the potential risks specific to the account balance of fixed assets to which your business may be exposed and what action would be appropriate to anticipate, mitigate and act on risk promptly.

Volume 2 "How to Manage Your Cash" explains some of the risk areas associated with the account balance of cash in the balance sheet and sets out examples of controls to minimise these risks. In addition, Lady Wise addresses how to better understand the cash that you have in your business on a daily basis and imparts her knowledge about the importance of cash flow forecasting and how to develop your forecasting skills to determine cash inflows and outflows as a tool for improved future business performance.

Volume 3 "How Well Do You Know Your Trade Debtors?" will help you to improve your understanding of the sales cycle and explain how to focus on trade debtors and avoid any potential over-statement of this important debtor account balance in the balance sheet.

Volume 4 "What Are Your Liabilities?" explains the importance of evaluating what are your liabilities in your business to provide you with as complete and accurate records as is possible giving you control and knowledge over the account balance of trade creditors or accounts payable to which they are often referred. This guidance will allow you to understand your creditors and know where your money is going in the business to meet various costs incurred.

Volume 5 "Are You Taking Stock?" focuses on the account balance of Stock in your business and includes learning about the general potential error types that can arise in managing stock and how to minimise the risk of them in your own business.

Volume 6 "M POWER!" evolved from the creation, narration and production of a collection of 45 video vignettes by Lady Wise.

Claim your Mastery and self-emPOWER!

This book addresses key business success factors that will improve your leadership skills as a foundation for accelerated business performance and sustainable business growth in the new era. Sounds like many other business books perhaps? What makes this so special?

What is especially intriguing is that in order to achieve the desired accelerated business performance, Lady Wise explains that the foundation for this joy and success has its grounding and roots immersed and melded first in the personal transformation of oneself!

Your Own Poetry

www.ingramcontent.com/pod-product-compliance
Lightning Source LLC
Chambersburg PA
CBHW071606030726
47593CB00001BA/334

* 9 7 8 0 9 9 3 3 5 1 3 6 5 *